There is a long Christian traditio
spend time preparing for the rea
impulse, but rather a wise atte
Drawing on scripture, insights from psychology, and uniting
truths, Tim Sisemore's book gently guides readers through the
complexity of dealing with death, grief, hope, and promise. In
these pages many will find real comfort and strength

KELLY M. KAPIC
author of *Embodied Hope: A Theological
Meditation on Pain and Suffering*

Woody Allen once said, "I am not afraid of death, I just don't
want to be there when it happens!" In a gentle and candid way,
Tim Sisemore prepares the reader to be very present when death
happens. As I read each chapter I wished I had this book decades
ago as a young pastor, ministering to the dying. I wished I had
this book when my younger brother and father died. There is rich
wisdom in these pages that echo wisdom from ages past when
dying and death could not be easily avoided. Most importantly,
this wisdom is grounded in the life, death and resurrection of
Jesus. Read Tim's book on death. It will make you more alive.

DR TIMOTHY S. LANE
President,
Institute for Pastoral Care

Timothy A. Sisemore

Finding God

While

Facing

Death

CHRISTIAN
FOCUS

Copyright © Timothy Sisemore 2017

paperback ISBN 978-1-5271-0024-4
epub ISBN 978-1-5271-0052-7
mobi ISBN 978-1-0053-4

10 9 8 7 6 5 4 3 2 1

Published in 2017
by
Christian Focus Publications Ltd,
Geanies House, Fearn, Ross-shire,
IV20 1TW, Great Britain.

www.christianfocus.com

Cover design by Paul Lewis

Printed and bound by
Bell and Bain, Glasgow

MIX
Paper from
responsible sources
FSC® C007785

Table of Contents

*To the memory
of my father and
grandmother, who
showed me how
to die well.*

Question 1:

WHAT IS YOUR ONLY COMFORT IN LIFE AND DEATH?

Answer:

That I am not my own, but belong – body and soul, in life and in death – to my faithful Savior Jesus Christ.

He has fully paid for all my sins with his precious blood, and has set me free from the tyranny of the devil. He also watches over me in such a way that not a hair can fall from my head without the will of my Father in heaven: in fact, all things must work together for my salvation.

Because I belong to him, Christ, by his Holy Spirit, assures me of eternal life and makes me whole-heartedly willing and ready from now on to live for him.

From the *Heidelberg Catechism*

Invitation to Our Study

You only live twice. Once when you are born and once when you look death in the face.

Ian Fleming
You Only Live Twice

What a strange quote to begin a study of finding God in death and dying! Yet it captures a vital truth that is often missed in our day. We spend much of our lives scurrying about as if there is no such thing as death. Like much of culture, our busyness shields us from the reality that we are all mortals. There is something inauthentic about this. To compare to the other 'inevitability' noted by Benjamin Franklin, it is like spending our money as though none of it need be saved for taxes. It will eventually catch up with you.

When we face death, we are more alive than ever in that we are being honest about who we are. We are sinful human beings, marked by the wages of sin: death (Rom. 6:23). To live with our heads in the sand about that reality is to miss out on what life really is. Facing death puts all of life and our faith into perspective – an eternal perspective. Though we are quick to acknowledge our belief about death and the fate of those who die, with or without Christ, there is a disconnect between what we say and how we live. As a result, facing death can open our eyes to this.

Many who read this will be in the throes of facing death directly, whether it is your own life or that of a loved one that is in jeopardy. Others will come to this book after having lost a loved one, whether after a prolonged illness or more suddenly. Others may pick this up in order to be better equipped to serve loved ones who grieve. Some may just read out of an interest in the topic.

Whatever brings us together, we share our mortality. It is not a matter of whether, but when. In researching, thinking, and writing this book, my increased awareness of our mortality has indeed made me feel 'alive' in a way I have not before. I sense more seriousness in how I approach each day and what I think of and how I treat others. I find myself clinging a little more carefully to God, or – more accurately – being more comforted by being held securely in His embrace. Of course, I write as one who has not been through my own death, but that is a weakness shared by any who write on the topic.

It is a good thing to think about and meditate upon dying and death, for it puts our lives in the larger context of God's work and His plans for us, both in the short and long terms. I thank God that you are willing to step into this study.

This little book is not intended to give all the answers, nor to serve as a how-to book about facing death. Rather, I have designed it to be a series of relatively brief meditations on a variety of aspects of death and dying. Given our tendency to hide from this or to live as though we won't die, I hope we are guided to a closeness to the God who is not hidden from us, but we from Him. God is with us in death and dying, and we find Him by stepping from behind our fears and realizing He is with us already.

Our study is written for the groups mentioned above: those who are facing their own deaths, those who have a loved one dying, those who are bereaved, those who minister to the bereaved, and those who simply care to understand the issue a bit better. As each situation is unique, not every chapter will be relevant to every reader. Nor will there be a chapter to cover every need, for each will have unique challenges in his or her life in the face of death. I invite you to read straight through, or pick and choose topics that seem more relevant to your current situation.

I desire that each chapter serve to stimulate your thinking, and in turn, your praying. It is not intended to be read in one sitting. First, because I assume if you are facing your own or a loved one's death, you will not be able to sit for a while to read it. But second, these topics are weighty emotionally and spiritually. Seek God's guidance before and as you read. Pause during and after each chapter to meditate on what you have read, seeking the Spirit's wisdom to understand and to respond as would please God. Pray based on what you discern. Worship and wonder before God. Lament and wrestle with God. Confess your sins and your failures. Ask for courage to reach out to others based on what you learn. Serve and love others in light of what you learn. Know more and more that you belong to a God who sent His Son to face death – and in so doing, to overcome it.

In Part I, we will reflect on how death is understood and even avoided in our modern culture. We will also survey what the Bible teaches us about death and dying, and how we are to live in light of that. Part II is offered to those who are realizing that a loved one is likely going to die soon. Not all have the luxury of preparing for a loved one's death, and support and guidance are provided to those who have the chance to walk through dying with a loved one. Part III is primarily for those who are dying and have the strength of mind, soul, and body, to contemplate the final days to come and their aftermath. Part IV draws attention to the special tragedy of deaths out of season: those who die before they are old and children who lose loved ones. These are especially bitter providences that merit particular attention. In Part V we consider the grief and mourning process after a loved one dies, offering some thoughts on how to walk through this valley and to accompany others who are doing so.

I feel strangely more alive after writing this as I better feel my place in God's plan. I pray that reading and meditating on these things will also be used in your life, to make you feel more alive to God as you sense His presence more openly as you walk the valley of the shadow of death.

Part I

Death and Dying in the 21st Century

Introduction

Things are changing. They are changing in the world around us, and changing for you as you or a loved one looks into the face of the last enemy: death (1 Cor. 15:26). How Christians look at and approach death has changed, too. Today we have so much hope in modern medicine to prolong life. At the same time, we live in a world that denies death and avoids taking it seriously. Even in our churches, we may avoid serious discussion of death. But the time comes when we cannot avoid it any longer.

In our first section, we will look at modern attitudes about death, both in general and particularly among Christians. We will look at culture and then at the Bible to see what we can learn about death and the life after death. This section is relevant for any who wish to reflect on what Scripture teaches on the subject, and how that fits into modern attitudes about death and dying.

1
The Lost Art of Dying Christianly

Therefore, since we are surrounded by so great a cloud of witnesses, let us also lay aside every weight, and sin which clings so closely, and let us run with endurance the race that is set before us, looking to Jesus, the founder and perfecter of our faith, who for the joy that was set before him endured the cross, despising the shame, and is seated at the right hand of the throne of God.

HEBREWS 12:1-2

Strangely, as I begin to write a book on dying I am thinking of a particular church in my community. In an effort to relate to and reach people in the current culture, it meets in a movie theater – a real, live, operating movie theater. I guess there are advantages to this: you don't have to buy a building, the seats are comfortable, and you have an awesome screen onto which to project the lyrics to praise songs. Yet, it seems to me that churches in days gone by had other advantages. Apart from a greater sense of focus on God and a location in the midst of the community, an unexpected benefit for many of these older churches is the presence of a cemetery next to the building. Members of the family of God would be laid to rest beside the place where they had worshiped Him, and near those with whom they had gathered to seek the Lord. In more settled and stable communities, worshipers would walk past the graves of parents, grandparents, spiritual mentors, and other departed saints as they walked to worship the same God in the same place where these revered ones had. The thoughtful worshiper would be reminded of death each time he or she walked toward the sanctuary – and of the hope found in the God he or she worships.

I am struck by the contrast of the movie theater church. Going to worship means passing popcorn stands, posters touting upcoming films (often with images on them that would be considered lewd and evil by our Christian forebears), and an atmosphere of pleasure and indulgence in the culture. The movies shown the night before would graphically depict the deaths of many nameless characters, their fate met with approval if not laughter. In other movies, physical and earthly pleasures are the staple, interspersed with crass language and humor, much of which stands in direct violation of the third commandment.

Nothing here hints that we ourselves face death and if anything, it associates worship with the entertainment going on in the auditorium the rest of the week. This feels more like escape from life's realities than a way of dealing with them. Again, I see the strategic idea behind this and there are undoubtedly some advantages. Yet, it supports the modern culture's avoidance of and trivialization of life's most basic reality: we will all die one day. No question of if, but only of when.

The irony of the church's drift toward the temporal is that the Christian church originates in the story of the most unjust and tragic death in history. Our hope is in Jesus whose death paid the price for our sins. But it is also in the incomparable hope of the resurrection from the dead. To be Christian is to be enthralled with and encouraged by that hope. The cemetery serves as a visible sign that yes, we'll die, too, but the sanctuary next door is a place to celebrate the hope that awaits those who die in the Lord. For those who knew those buried there, there is a reverence and memory for lives well lived, lives of faith that met challenges with grace and hope – of forbears of our faith who have received the rewards of the faithful as described in Hebrews 11.

In contrast, our culture conspires to keep our minds from seriously considering our mortality. Many movies in the theater will depict thousands of deaths of nameless, faceless minor characters whose demise serves only to amuse us. Even the death of others is entertainment so long as we don't take it very seriously. In fact, it serves as a release of our own anxieties about mortality by distancing us from our inevitable deaths. Only a few rare movies show the true nature of death and its impact on those close to the deceased.

But the culture 'protects' us in other ways. Even the deaths of the animals we eat are hidden from us. I still recall in my childhood that we bought a half of a pig from relatives who lived on a farm. It was the only time I actually met my food while it was still alive (excepting a couple of lobsters here and there). This made eating that pig a bit strange – and I was certainly not around to see it slaughtered! Most of us are in the same situation: we eat meat but never see the animal alive that gave its life for our dinner.

Take this thought a step further. Imagine living in Old Testament times when every day would be accentuated with the squeals and yelps of animals being sacrificed and the smells of the burnt offerings. A walk near the Temple would expose you to the crimson residue of the blood shed in the sacrifices. I wonder how much more vivid my sense of the cost of my sin would have been in that setting.

We are also unique in history in our lack of exposure to death. Through most of history, death was earlier and more common. Parents would almost expect that one or more of their children would die, tragedies experienced even by Christian leaders such as Martin Luther. While most of us experience the loss of a loved one when we're young, it is not as common as before.

However, maybe one of the most subtle ways we keep our distance from death is by the modern philosophy of medicine and care in hospitals. I thank God for the great progress medicine has made in extending our lives and making them more comfortable. Writing today at age sixty, I have outlived the average life expectancy of a person one-hundred years ago by ten years already! We should be grateful for the progress we've seen because of modern medicine.

Yet, the progress of medicine has been so dramatic that now we almost see dying as a form of losing a battle – a metaphor often heard among Christians. We throw everything we have at disease and, as a result, often isolate a dying person from family and Christian community in the confines of a hospital. Sixty-three per cent of Americans die in hospitals, with an additional 17 per cent dying in institutions such as nursing homes. That leaves only 20 per cent dying elsewhere, and we assume not all of those die at home. Yet historically, home was the common place for death as it afforded a chance for loved ones and church family to gather around the dying person as they transitioned from this earthly life. And burial would be near the spiritual home of the person, the church.

A major reason behind this movement to care in institutions is the eagerness to fight for life. Emboldened by medical progress, we resist letting go of loved ones and go to extremes to preserve life. Most churches today have prayer lists that read as though health and life were the only things we value and implore God about. I must be careful, for this is only human after all. We naturally resist dying and fight for life.

Christians, though, claim that there is a better life after this one, one free from sin and suffering as we know it in this world. We agree with the apostle Paul when he proclaims, 'to die is gain' (Phil. 1:21), yet somehow we struggle to treat death as gain. I often wonder whether God is always honored in our prayers to preserve life rather than for him to be glorified in death. Admittedly, the balance is a challenging one to strike: knowing as Paul did also that 'to live is Christ'. It seems that the balance mostly tips toward valuing this life over the next, and I'm not sure that honors God as it should, for recall that Paul goes on to say that 'my desire is to depart and be with Christ, for that is far better' (v. 23).

Do we really believe that? If so, why do we strive so to keep ourselves and our loved ones alive on this earth? Why do we turn death into some type of medical failure rather than attribute death to the will of God and a joyous event for believers? How are we to navigate a culture that hides from and denies death when Christians have a much richer view of things?

Barring the return of our Lord, you and I will both die. We likely will see loved ones do the same. How are we to navigate this perplexing gauntlet between wanting to preserve life yet holding fast to the truths of eternal life? These are some of the questions we will address in the pages that follow as we seek a fresh perspective on death in light of the gospel of Christ.

I can't say that it is wrong for Christians to worship in movie theaters, but I do know that we struggle to keep a Christian view of death in the midst of a culture that denies it. We would honor the dead and the dying, as did the author of Hebrews, by drawing courage and hope from this great cloud of witnesses. Join me in reflecting on some topics that will refresh our souls as we consider the journey from this world to the next where we and our loved ones will join that great cloud of witnesses.

2
The Denial of Death

But the serpent said to the woman,
'You will not surely die.'

GENESIS 3:4

The quote above comes from a very famous context. Adam and Eve were immortal. Death would not befall them … unless, unless they ate of the fruit of the tree that God had prohibited. The serpent challenges God's promise of death to them should they disobey. As we all know, they did, and now all die.

Today we still try to believe the words of the serpent, yet in a different way. We take our fear of dying and shove it to the background with distraction and with misdirection. A century ago it was taboo to talk about anything having to do with sex. But after Freud there has been a steady move to where sex is discussed quite openly in all kinds of settings – even in the early years of schooling for children. The new taboo is death, and we avoid discussing it today much as we avoided discussing sex years ago.

We hinted at some of the ways this happens in our first chapter. We hide death and do our best to make believe it isn't there. We don't see our food killed nor do we have to consider those who died as cemeteries are not as present as in the past. The conspiracy runs deeper, though. Let's consider three main ways people in modern life deny death.

Distraction is our most common defense against thoughts of death. We keep busier than any previous generation. Even if not working, we are texting, communicating on social media, watching media on television or our computers, or involved in games or other activities that occupy our minds. Even a few minutes of standing in a queue leads to impatience and a need for distraction. Sometimes one thing isn't enough, so we 'multi-task' to busy our minds.

Psychology suggests many purposes in keeping so busy and many things we are thus trying to avoid, but none of these are as basic as avoiding the fact that we will die. My thick, dark hair is now salt and pepper colored. The Bible (e.g., Prov. 16:31) tells me that this gray hair is a 'crown of glory', but my television reminds me that it makes me look old, and to be old is to be closer to death. I am advised, then, to dye it so as to look younger. Other advertisements challenge me that older adults can still do very athletic things (if we partake of their products). Don't think you're getting older (and nearer death), you're getting better. Speak to the contrary, and you may be told not to 'talk like that'. I enjoy shocking some of my classes by saying simply that my gray hair tells me I'm getting closer to the day of my death. Try talking that way and watch the discomfort you can cause!

'You're only as old as you feel', 'sixty is the new forty' and other platitudes help us avoid the realities that we are advancing in age toward the day of our death. As we will see later, our almost worshipful outlook on medicine leads us to believe that it can cure all ills and lead us to the perpetual fountain of youth. Keep hoping and maybe you won't die – or at least won't until a very, very old age.

Younger folks avoid the realities of death sometimes by avoiding contact with those who are dying. More than half of those living in nursing homes have no family that visit. 'Out of sight, out of mind' helps the younger generations avoid the unpleasantries of advancing age and the approach of death. Not witnessing death through our lives leaves us unprepared for the difficulties of walking through the dying days of loved ones. Parents may 'protect' their young children by 'sparing' them visits to see great-grandma in the nursing home, helping insulate them from death's inevitability.

But the fear of death is in us all, and won't go quietly into the night. So, we have to defeat it by teasing it.

Minimization of death is another cultural way of denying death. Minimizing is a way of taking something and trying to make it 'no big deal'. Minimizing death is a way to make us feel power over it or to make it trivial. Maybe no better example exists than the traditional and numerous James Bond films where numerous henchmen are killed off in each movie, with the viewer trained to care little if not even laugh at some of their fates. Star Trek was famous for the nameless crewmember who would go down to planets. As soon as the viewer noticed that an unknown person was a member of the landing party, you knew the person's fate was assured.

Sometimes, more maliciously, death is played for entertainment value. The viewer of the drama is supposed to 'enjoy' graphic violence to persons leading to their death. Special effects can make such suffering gruesome and in so doing, increase profits of the program or video game. Not just movies, but video games push the limits of graphic violence in order to sell products. After all, we know it isn't real.

But maybe the most basic minimization approach in our culture is our view of heroes – again, particularly in the media. Ernest Becker, in his non-fiction Pulitzer Prize Winner *The Denial of Death*, sees the hero as the embodiment of the fear of death. We identify with the hero and want to be one. And the key? Facing death without fear and overcoming it. The hero challenges the odds and does great deeds without dying in the process. This plays well to those wishing to defy the odds to live.

Mass media exploits this theme as heroes in the movies routinely overcome huge odds and defy death repeatedly and with flair. The scenarios of such heroism move beyond the improbable to the absurd as single heroes ward off dozens of would-be killers who somehow lack wisdom to hide or talent to aim. We abandon our reason at the door so we can be engrossed in such overblown success against the odds. (And yes, we're expected to be humored or excited by the deaths of those who would take down our hero.) Even as I write, an image of the old Superman television program comes to mind, with our hero standing smugly and defiantly as multiple bullets harmlessly bounce off his chest. Wouldn't we all like to be like that?

In short, culture not only seeks to distract us from our anxieties about death (and we all too often oblige), it offers stories that support the idea that we will somehow transcend death by being heroic. The irony should not be lost on Christians: we serve a Savior who is our hero not because He avoided death, but because He actually overcame it. Similarly, the heroes of Hebrews 11 are esteemed because of their faith – with the author of Hebrews specifically pointing out that death preceded the reward for many of them.

Finally, people in contemporary culture steel themselves against the inevitability of death by seeking to avoid it by **prevention** – or at least delaying it as long as possible. I want to be careful here: we all need to do what we can to be healthy – good diet and exercise and all. Yet, it is not hard to become obsessed with health beyond what is healthy. I am not the person to say where the line should be drawn, but maybe it is more about the reasoning behind it.

Seeking to be healthy is commendable, but any thought that health is a way to avoid death is misguided. It may not even postpone death. Many people still recall the tragic death of Jim Fixx whose 1977 book ignited the running revolution. This expert who practiced what he preached died from a heart attack at age 52 just after jogging. Obsessing about health can give us a false sense of security about our longevity, making us feel some sense of control over our death (and that is one of the most powerful psychological concerns about death: we can't control it). At best we increase the odds of a longer life, but only God knows when it will be our time to die.

I recall working with a certain woman when I was counseling people in nursing homes. She had led a productive, God-fearing life and was leaving a legacy of a wonderful family who were assets to the community and who cared about her. Yet, she had terminal cancer and was not far from death. Her nursing staff complained to me that she was becoming uncooperative as they pushed her to eat and do other things to prolong her life. As I spoke with her, she responded well to my empathy when I commented on how the staff didn't understand that she just wanted to 'go home' to be with her Savior. Her peace at the end of a race well-run was a testimony to her faith and exposed the more common view that you have to fight intensely to defeat the enemy of death.

She faced her death more openly than the staff who cared for her. This woman's faith shows that looking head-on at the inevitability of death is healthy, even (and especially) when the body is not. Her story foreshadows our discussion of the medicalization of death, the final product of our efforts of prevention. Our boundless faith in medicine leads us to hope that all things will be cured and to die is to disservice the field of medicine in some way.

Prayerfully reflect on your life and attitudes toward death. How has the culture impacted you? How do you distract yourself from the realities of your death and the death of those you love? Do you resist the imminent death of a loved one or even yourself? As we begin our journey of meditations on Christian death and dying, let us be honest with ourselves and each other. We will die, and the only question is when. For Christians, it is only a mysterious passage to the 'gain' Paul anticipated in his own death when he stated that 'to die is gain' (Phil. 1:21).

3
Living for the Here and Hereafter

For now we see in a mirror dimly, but then face to face.
Now I know in part; then I shall know fully, even
as I have been fully known.

1 CORINTHIANS 13:12

Modern life is great for many of us. Probably at no time in history can so many people enjoy so many things in life. For most of us in the West, we have never known what it is like to be truly hungry, even insulting those who do when we make such blithe comments as 'I'm starving'. We have wonderful health care that can cure many ailments and make us reasonably comfortable with others. Most who work have jobs that are nothing like the miserable hours and conditions that many of our forebears experienced. We have microwaves and fast foods so we can eat in a hurry; televisions, smart phones, and the Internet keep us informed and entertained constantly. We communicate as swiftly with people on the other side of the globe as we do those who live next door. And for the most part, we know little or nothing about being persecuted for our faith.

We live in a world made by our loving God, amid resplendent beauty in nature surrounding us. We also have the blessings of music, art, companionship, and food. We need not be worldly in a secular sense to have pleasure in this world. And that is not to mention the spiritual joys with which God blesses His children. Daily we know that God is with us and watches over us.

This is all cause for giving thanks to God. These are, in general, blessings. But they may carry a hidden problem with them. They can make us feel too comfortable in a world that is sinful and godless. We can easily take on the values of the culture around us and then turn to God to ask Him to give us an advantage in obtaining them. God will bless our hard work with prosperity, for example, or bless our children with good educations and jobs. In short, we can become so earthly minded that our faith is merely a resource to make life here better as we seek the same goals as our non-Christian neighbors do. Spiritual blessings are to be an 'appetizer' for what awaits after this life, not the 'main course' of what life is about.

This trend is strangely evident in how many Christians pray. Most church prayer lists are for members who are sick, and our prayers are generally aimed at seeking God's mercy to heal them from their various maladies. I must be careful here, for this is a subtle point. Illness and death are not the way creation operated prior to the sin in the Garden of Eden. They are not to be celebrated by any means and we, of course, seek to be healthy and to prolong our earthly lives. But then again, who doesn't?

How might a Christian be different in this regard? After all, if you are a secularist, this life is it. Make the most of it; milk it for all it is worth. When it is finished, so are you. All of the pleasure, meaning, and fulfillment that one can accrue have to occur now. Therefore, now is the time for pleasure, health, and security.

But Christians see things differently. We are to live our lives in such a way that they look silly if there is no resurrection. Paul says as much in 1 Corinthians 15:19: 'If in Christ we have hope in this life only, we are of all people most to be pitied.' The Gospel is not just something to make this life better (though it certainly does that by restoring a relationship with our Creator). The Christian hope, rather, is seen in the hereafter. Scripture promises us hardship and turmoil here. We are in a spiritual warfare (remember the discussion of this in relation to the armor of God in Eph. 6?), and that is grueling. Recall in the hall of faith in Hebrews 11 that many of the heroes underwent great hardships and died without realizing the blessings of faith. Jesus himself walked right into a horrifying death, doing so because of 'the joy that was set before him' (Heb. 12:2).

In the abundance of our blessings we can be tempted to think we are in heaven here on earth and not want to leave. Even our illnesses and troubles can serve as helpful reminders that this is not our destiny as Christians. We are promised a day when our Savior will dry every tear from our eyes (Rev. 21:4), and that day will not come on the present earth. We are given a hope for something better on the other side of death.

For many in church history, this hope was called the beatific vision: the beautiful day when we will see God face-to-face, as it were, as Paul tells us in 1 Corinthians 13:12. We don't understand life, and we don't understand death. Suffering is everywhere, and we struggle to find its meaning. But through all of this there is the hope that we will see Jesus someday. That hope sustained the heroes of faith as we saw, and is to inspire us now.

Our comforts may compromise our longing for heaven and the life that awaits. We may be just satisfied enough with our lives and our many creature comforts that it keeps us from hungering for the life to come. That is a contrast with people like Paul who saw dying to be gain (Phil. 1:21), even as he valued life for the sake of spreading the Gospel.

Maybe we need to re-assess our definition of 'blessing' a bit. Maybe the many comforts and pleasures of this world, especially those related to entertainment, are not really blessings. Maybe they give us just enough satisfaction to quell the natural longing of the Christian to be with the Lord. If that is so, they may be more of a trick of the devil than a blessing from the Father.

Of course, we don't have to choose really. We can enjoy God's good things now (if we are careful that they are God's good things and not sinful pleasures fed by greed and selfishness). But we must not think this is the goal of it all. If we are living biblically, these good things are temporal respites from the war against Satan. Maybe we don't suffer as much because we aren't stepping into the battle as God would have us.

And in so doing, maybe the beatific vision has blurred. For some people who are so enamored of earthly pleasures, I wonder if eternity with Christ even sounds good. For believers who know their Bible and are stepping into obedience, despite its hardships, the hereafter should sound wonderful. We think of the present too much; we think of the future too little. We are enticed by physical pleasures of the now and unacquainted with the rich spiritual joys of the future.

Let us pray for those who are sick, but maybe pray also that they will have a greater clarity of the beatific vision, and a longing to go home to be with Jesus and be freed from a sinful world of suffering. As we look at death ourselves, or walk through its shadow with loved ones, let us consider that being healed may be the second best option. If we read the stories of martyrs of the faith, very often even in the midst of suffering there was glory in their eyes – the hope of the freedom and joy that was just ahead. After all, if this life is all we have, we are no different from those without faith. Maybe if those without faith saw our hope in the face of death, Christianity would be more understandable.

4

Living (and Dying) in Light of the Resurrection

I protest, brothers, by my pride in you, which I have in Christ Jesus our Lord, I die every day! What do I gain if, humanly speaking, I fought with beasts at Ephesus? If the dead are not raised, 'Let us eat and drink, for tomorrow we die.'

1 CORINTHIANS 15:31-32

Thinking about death and dying can be unsettling. As we've seen, it is tempting to get wrapped up in this life so as to avoid thinking about the next. Yet, as we think about human mortality, it pushes us to consider the importance of the resurrection in our lives here on earth. We will reflect on what this means to us who are living, and then consider implications for those who are dying.

It is a common feature among modern Western Christians to see faith as useful more than transformative. What I mean by that is we see being Christian as helpful to us in many ways, enabling us to live our lives better than those without Christ. We can pray about the job interview, find consolation when things don't go our way, and even take pleasure in worship and fellowship. For all we said about the Lordship of Christ, more often we treat Him as One who loves us and makes us feel better … maybe more like a divine therapist than the Son of God. We live our lives with goals, ambitions, pleasures, and emotions that don't look very different from those around us. We want a nicer house, better pay, good health, winsome children, and so forth. But we are glad we have Jesus, too.

Paul's writings make clear that the Christian faith is much more than this. 1 Corinthians 15 speaks much of the resurrection of Christ and its implications for those who follow the Savior. The gist of it is that all of our lives are to be lived so that our lives are senseless if Christ is not risen. In Paul's words (v. 19), 'If in Christ we have hope in this life only, we are of all people most to be pitied.' The real hope is what Christ's resurrection affords us in the afterlife. The hope of the glorious resurrection bodies described in verses 42-49 not only takes the sting and victory away from death (v. 55), it gives us an entirely new outlook on this life.

What does living in light of the resurrection look like? We will borrow from an essay by John Piper[1] to outline Paul's argument in this chapter.

The Resurrection makes us Less Fearful in Life

First, the hope of resurrection we have based on Christ's resurrection makes us less fearful in life so that we more willingly face dangers for the sake of the Gospel. Paul lists travel dangers (he was an itinerant missionary, after all), dangers from robbers, from Jews and Gentiles, in the city or in the country (wilderness), and from false brothers. Faith inherently involves some risk. When I trust the chair I am sitting in, I have faith it will hold me up so I commit my entire body to be dependent on its faithfulness. Faith that we have hope in the next life moves us to trust God more in this one and take chances on behalf of the Gospel. Wonder what chances you might take if your faith in the resurrection were like Paul's?

Paul was consumed by the cause of the Gospel, so much so that he really embodied the words 'to live is Christ'. He denied his own rights and aspirations for the sake of the Gospel. 2 Corinthians 11:23b-27 lists among the things he accepted; greater labors, many imprisonments, countless beatings, being brought near to death, whippings, beatings, a stoning, three shipwrecks, and being adrift

---

1. John Piper (2007), *The Radical Effects of the Resurrection*, last accessed 02/07/2017 at http:desiringgod.org/articles/radical-effects-of-the-resurrection

at sea for a day and a night. More than these, he worked so hard for the sake of the kingdom that he lost sleep, was hungry and thirsty, went without food, and was exposed to the elements. Beyond all of this, he felt daily pressure to care for the churches he worked with. Clearly, Paul did not do this for earthly gain and if Christ is only about this life, Paul indeed was pitiable. Elsewhere in his writings we read of his dealing with frequent opposition to the Gospel, both from outside the church and in it. Rather than avoid it, the Apostle embraced it as his mission in this life, awaiting the glory of the next.

In contrast, if death was the end of it all, we might as well just party. This is, of course, the philosophy of the world – have a good time while you can. Enjoy your life and your money for you can't take it with you. Maybe some of our dread of death is due to imbibing more of this worldview than we like to think.

Paul chose obedience and so chose suffering. If you recall, suffering was actually part of the 'job description' he received in Acts 9:16. His hope in the resurrection caused him to look past the sufferings of this life to the joys of the next. It freed him from the love of things and money. He knew his reward awaiting him after this life ended.

I can do no better at this point than to quote Piper:

> *This is a radical call for us to look hard at our present lives to see if they are shaped by the hope of the resurrection. Do we make decisions on the basis of gain in this world or gain in the next? Do we take risks for love's sake that can only be explained as wise if there is a resurrection?*

As you face the death of a loved one or reflect on your own mortality, prayerfully consider how God would have you live today. What might you do to make it clear, like Paul, that your faith is about more than worldly comfort? How might you be an example to others in this regard?

The Resurrection makes us Less Fearful in Death

Finally, what does this passage say to those who are in the throes of the dying process? Maybe you are aging, or coping with cancer, or another terminal illness? We are all closer to death today than we've ever been. Even today I learned that a hearing loss I had hoped was temporary is apparently permanent. I grieve this little loss, but then again, this inspires me to hope of the resurrection and to make the most of the days I have to live for Christ.

The great early church father Athanasius wrote of the power of the death and resurrection of Christ in the lives of believers in his day and before, and how the hope of resurrection transformed them, particularly as it showed how Christ had defeated death:

> *When a tyrant has been defeated by a real king, and bound hand and foot, then all that pass by laugh him to scorn, buffeting and reviling him, no longer fearing his fury and barbarity, because of the king who has conquered him; so also, death having been conquered and exposed by the Saviour on the Cross, and bound hand and foot, all they who are in Christ, as they pass by, trample on him, and witnessing to Christ scoff at death, jesting at him, and saying what has been written against him of old: 'O death, where is thy victory? O grave, where is thy sting.'[2]*

We, too, can be testimonies to the Gospel in how we die, showing to those around us that '… we do not lose heart. Though our outer self is wasting away, our inner self is being renewed day by day. For this light momentary affliction is preparing for us an eternal weight of glory beyond all comparison' (2 Cor. 4:16-17). If you are seriously ill, consider how you, too, can serve, by modeling faith and living out the hope of the resurrection – by not losing heart. You can still pray, can still read the Bible (I assume that if you are reading these words), can still meditate on God's goodness and the wonderful life that waits you after this 'light momentary affliction'. Suffering will pass, but life will be full and joyful when we join Christ in the resurrection. Praise be to His Name!

---

2. From Athanasius, *On the Incarnation of the Word*, S:28.

5

The Medicalization of Death and Dying

[Death] makes its power felt ... in a hospital when medicine neglects the community and the voice of the patient.

ALLEN VERHEY[1]

One of the dangers of our age is to be so caught up in our own cultures and traditions that we lose historical perspective. It probably isn't wise to assume that 'new is better' and how we do things these days is better than ever. Just because folks in the past didn't have the technology we have doesn't mean they lacked wisdom. In fact, it may be that they were wiser in some ways *because* they lacked our technology.

Dealing with a dying person is a great example of this complexity. I will illustrate my points by briefly painting two word pictures.

First, I offer a modern day picture of the severely ill person. Carol (let us call her) is in her early 90s and is weakening from the complications of diabetes and heart disease. Unable to feed herself well and becoming less mobile, her physicians urge her family to put her in a hospital so she can receive intravenous fluids and round-the-clock nursing care. So as not to stress her, the family is asked to limit their time with her and to minimize

---

1. *The Christian Art of Dying: Learning from Jesus* (Grand Rapids, MI: Eerdmans), 2011; p. 20.

visitors. As Carol continues to weaken, her pain increases and the hospital staff puts her on strong pain medications that render her almost unconscious. She can hardly interact with her family. Her family and her church community diligently pray for her healing and recovery, hoping against hope that she will gain strength, overcome infection, and be able to return home. One night as her family was home, Carol slips into unconsciousness and dies – alone in her hospital room.

Now, let's go back, say 200 years, to compare how this might have unfolded then. Elizabeth is in her 50s and has contracted serious pneumonia. Too weak to walk and carry on her normal activities, she is confined to a bed and cared for by her family. Her physician visits on occasion, but it is clear that her days are few. Family and church members are with her constantly, conversing when she is stronger, simply being present to Elizabeth when she is sleeping or too weak to talk. She has a brief conversation with a neighbor, asking forgiveness for the time she lost her temper with this valued friend. Elizabeth's children and grandchildren each realize this matriarch is dying, and are careful to share with her their love and appreciation. In turn, Elizabeth confirms her love to each and offers a charge to keep the faith. A leader of the church prays with her and comforts her by reading Scripture. Her loved ones draw near as does the end of Elizabeth's earthly life. She dies surrounded by her loved ones.

I admit I've stereotyped these two stories a bit, but I did so to help make some important points. Death used to be most commonly caused by an infectious disease and without antibiotics and other medications, these were often fatal. This is a major reason that our life expectancies have increased in recent history. Without the mixed blessings of modern medicine, all involved knew that such an illness would likely be fatal. The family and faith community of the ill person conspired to comfort the dying person as she completed her suffering and transitioned to the presence of God. Death was a communal event.

Today, we have won enough victories over disease that we are optimistic that illness can be defeated – even maybe overly optimistic. Deaths now are often even more gradual and are due to chronic diseases such as cardiovascular illness, diabetes, or cancer. The victories of medicine have made us able to live longer with such illnesses, but have also made us tenacious, clinging to the hope of living forever. We are more likely today to pray for healing and life than to work on comforting the dying person, getting closure, and surrendering the loved one to the grace of God that offers eternal life. The old model sees death as the inevitable end of earthly life and a transition into eternal life. The medicalized model sees death as a defeat of some sort.

An illustration of this comes from my own experience of counseling persons in nursing homes. A woman I recall had terminal cancer but was a strong Christian with a loving family and supportive church community. Her days were clearly numbered and few. Even as I would approach her bedside to be with her for a while, her nurses would exhort me to challenge her to eat better and fight her disease. I recall once near her last day simply approaching her after some of these medical staff comments and saying 'You just want to go home, don't you?' We both knew what 'home' meant for my sister in Christ.

You see, she was dying, not sick. Medicine gives us a 'sick' role even in our final illness. We fight against conceding that a person is dying, hoping against hope for some medical miracle if not a special intervention of God. I think the worst part of this is the dying person can then feel like a failure – not cooperating with the prayers of loved ones or the interventions of the medical profession.

This shift also moves the location of dying from home to the hospital. As recently as the 1940s only about 40 per cent of deaths in the US occurred in hospitals whereas now that number tops 90 per cent. Granted that the hospice movement (formed in reaction to the medicalization we're talking about) has helped, but still we focus on last-ditch medical care over communal care in many cases.

The other thing this accomplishes is to move death from our sights. Deaths occur out of the community in the hospital, so we aren't as directly exposed to them. We might visit a hospital, but not spend considerable time there as we might in a home. This is especially true for family members.

This also shifts our view of God's role in all of this. Most often we appeal to God to spare life and hope our faith will see the loved one (or oneself) through the sickness to health. Research does show that faith leads to longer lives overall (largely through promoting healthier lifestyles). Another study found that Christians fought harder against dying than did non-believers, taking on more aggressive treatments, failing to make advance directives for end-of-life care, and ultimately not dying well as a result.

Our prayers shift away from comfort to petitions for healing. Death is an enemy, for sure. But in Christ it is a defeated one that should lack 'sting'. But it stings more when we are fighting so hard against it and we may even become bitter against God for allowing it.

If we think for a moment, there is a strange paradox. For all Christians' belief about eternal life with God, we want to cling to this earthly life desperately. Why is this? One reason might be that we may share the earthly values of the culture and be so focused on happiness here that we neglect the eternal hope of the Gospel.

However, I suspect the larger reason is that we lack a deep faith in what eternity brings. We talk of it less in our churches so we greet death with a greater degree of ignorance than Elizabeth would have. Our churches too often offer so many prayers for life that they fail to teach people how to die in Christ.

Dying should ideally be a time for community, affording those affiliated with the dying person occasion to make peace, seek reconciliation, say final goodbyes, and prayerfully entrust the loved one to God's eternal care and protection. While this can be done in a hospital, it requires a focus on dying, not on extreme efforts to extend life. If eternity with Christ is what we believe it to be, why would we pray to extend a loved one's time on this earth (so long as the loved one is a believer in Christ)?

I invite you to rethink your attitudes about medicine and dying. We thank God for the many miracles of medicine and the years of life it affords us. Yet, as Christians, we view this in a larger context of an eternity of bliss with God. We need to stand against an unbelieving culture in this regard. In doing so, we can testify to the Gospel in death as well as in life.

6

What Happens When a Person Dies?

No one who questions death has experienced it, because it lies beyond experience. And no one who has experienced death can be questioned about it!

Ray S. Anderson[1]

Death is frightening for many reasons. It is not under our control, and most anxiety stems from feeling a lack of control. We don't know if we'll live to be 100 or die in an auto accident today. It is a most uncertain thing and we may exercise and eat right, but we still lack control.

But more than just being out of our control, death resists our curiosity. As the epigram above accurately observes, we have no first-hand accounts of death to draw from. Lazarus and Jesus are the only examples we have, and they give us little insight into exactly what happens when we die. The Bible itself is not as direct and clear as we would like.

So, the uncertainty of what happens at death is one of the major challenges of facing death. There may be some comfort in briefly considering some of what we can determine from the biblical references to death and an overall theology of death. You'll notice there are no 'proof texts' for this as one has to look at the references to terms like body and soul in Scripture and combine bits and pieces

---

1. *Theology, Death, and Dying* (New York, NY: Basil Blackwell), 1986; p. 3.

43

to form a theology. The following is, I believe, true to Scripture and its interpretation by the major fathers of the church.

What Are We Made of?

Let's begin with a debate in theology that is happening right now. What are we made of? That is, are we physical, spiritual, or both? Some theologians, enamored of the new brain science, say brain scans show no physical signs that we are more than physical beings. They conclude that we are bodies and have no souls. If they are right (and I don't think they are), we die with our bodies and will not know anything until the resurrection when our bodies are renewed. This position leaves Jesus's words to the thief on the cross, about being with Him, 'today you will be with me in Paradise' (Luke 23:43), as rather odd. The implication seems to be that the thief could anticipate something that day, not when the general resurrection occurs.

Most Christians in church history have held that we are body and soul, the dualist position. While a group holds that we are body, soul, and spirit, they agree that there is a soul that lives past death, so we won't make an argument here. Rather, we will assume, with the major Reformed confessions that echo the majority of the church fathers, that humans consist of body and soul, the soul being the immaterial life within us that survives the death of the body. As we noted, the biblical data are not crystal clear, but a survey of the uses of the Hebrew and Greek words for 'soul' yields this conclusion.

Why Do We Die?

Death is separation from God, so Adam and Eve died immediately upon eating the fruit (fulfilling the promise of Genesis 2:17). If they had not eaten, they would not have died. But they did, and they died spiritually and eventually physically as well, passing the curse of death on to all who follow. Death, then, is not 'natural' in the sense that God made our first parents to be eternal should they not have sinned.

What Happens When We Die?

We all die, and are made of body and soul. Now the question is what happens at death? We will follow the Westminster Confession that states (Chapter 32),

The bodies of men, after death, return to dust, and see corruption; but their souls (which neither die nor sleep), having an immortal subsistence, immediately return to God who gave them. The souls of the righteous, being then made perfect in holiness, are received into the highest heavens, where they behold the face of God in light and glory, waiting for the full redemption of their bodies; and the souls of the wicked are cast into hell, where they remain in torments and utter darkness, reserved to the judgment of the great day. Besides these two places for souls separated from their bodies, the Scripture acknowledgeth none.

When our bodies die (and we will avoid the debate over exactly what 'death' is medically), our souls remain conscious apart from the body. For believers in Christ, they are present before the face of God in the highest heavens, yet await a full redemption when reunited with their bodies. This will occur at the general resurrection when Christ returns to earth at the second-coming. On the other hand, a most unpleasant fate awaits those who die apart from Christ and in their sin. They begin a misery that will continue when they, too, are reunited with their bodies.

It is comforting to think that those who die in Christ will be with God, though admittedly we struggle to understand what that is like since we are so connected to the physical. If God is spirit and so are the angels, we should be at home there even without bodies. We will have fellowship with our God, and thus it will be wonderful.

But the ultimate goal is to be in our resurrected bodies as we will be for eternity, just as Jesus rose bodily when he ascended to heaven. Our life then will be in the new heavens and earth, reigning with Christ. Free from sin and death, the joy of everlasting life awaits the believer in Christ.

Let's pull together the story. We are body and soul. We all die as we are sinners in Adam. When our body dies, our soul joins God in an intermediate state that is conscious and enjoys fellowship with God. Since this is spiritual, it is a bit difficult to picture in our minds. Suffice it to say that when a loved one dies, the Bible teaches that he or she is in immediate bliss in the presence of God, freed from the woes and sin of our bodies. This is cause to rejoice even in the midst of loss. Though their bodies may be laid in the grave, our loved ones' souls are safe with God Himself. What a joy and hope!

I recall the night my father died. He had struggled for many years with polyps on his vocal cords and over thirty surgeries left these so scarred he could hardly speak. He loved our Lord dearly and longed to join in the singing when he was at church. As I drove to be with my mother that night, I was overwhelmed with a sense of ecstasy that my father could now sing. Not in his body, mind you, but freely and spiritually in the presence of the God he adored. He will some day have a new body and sing in the body. For now, I take comfort in knowing he is worshiping our God more fully and freely than he ever did when bound to his body. That is truly soul music!

Let us rejoice together in the happy fate of those who die in Christ, even as we grieve their loss to us who remain.

7

What Will Life Be
Like After Death?[1]

*And I saw the holy city, new Jerusalem, coming
down out of heaven from God, prepared as a bride
adorned for her husband.*

REVELATION 21:2

I imagine that the Promised Land was hard for the ancient
Israelites to envision. All they had known was slavery and
suffering. And the way out of Egypt was scary. A trip across the
desert was not enough; Pharaoh's army was hot on their tails. They
went because of God's promise, not because they had researched
it on the Internet as the ideal place to establish a new nation. I'm
sure folks were frightened of the journey – particularly as they
were not so sure of what the destination was like. Even after forty
years of wandering, the crossing of the Jordan presented one last
intimidating obstacle.

The Bible story makes clear there is a parallel here with our
crossing the 'river' of death into the Promised Land of heaven.
Yet, we often don't seem too eager to get to the other side of
Jordan. There may be two reasons for that. First, unlike Israel, we
often have a comfortable existence and so struggle to surrender
a place that is familiar and fairly pleasant, as discussed in

---

1. Much of this chapter is adapted from Wilbur M. Smith's *The Biblical
Doctrine of Heaven*, published originally by Moody Press, 1968, last accessed
02/07/2017 at http://www.ccel.us/doctrine.of.heaven.toc.html#6

chapter 3. It is not hard to become too comfortable here and not consider the better world that awaits us. Maybe one of the purposes of the challenges of old age and sickness is to loosen our love for this world and ready us to cross the Jordan to be with our Savior.

Calvin and others have stressed how we need to think much about our life in heaven with God. This gives us hope and reminds us every day that death is gain much more than it is loss. But with our busy and comfortable lives, we don't seem to think much on the topic. As a result, death may be scarier than it need be if we knew more of what awaits us. Let's consider that for a few minutes.

Where Will We Be?

The first question is where exactly will we be? Popular stories may have misled Christians a bit from what the Bible teaches on this topic. 'Heaven' is used in many ways and can refer to different things. This is illustrated by Paul's story of being caught up into the third heaven (2 Cor. 12:2), clearly implying there are two others. We won't get into detail here other than to point this out.

We saw earlier that our souls go to be with God while separated from the body. Since this is prior to the coming of the new heaven and new earth, we may assume this is in the heaven where the angels live. After the resurrection of the body, however, it appears we live in the New Jerusalem, or the holy city, as it is referred to in Revelation 21:2. Here is holiness and beauty, yet one could argue this isn't the same as heaven. The Holy Spirit apparently did not intend for us to understand this fully, but suffice it to say it will be a fantastic, beautiful, and sacred place where we will know happiness we've never known.

What Will it Be Like?

Our future life is one blessed beyond measure. First, Scripture tells us we have an inheritance (e.g., Matt. 25:34; 1 Pet. 1:3-5) that awaits us as the children of God. The Matthew text tells us that this inheritance is the kingdom itself, and Peter gives more detail by telling us the resurrection gives us hope of 'an inheritance that is imperishable, undefiled, and unfading, kept in heaven for you, who by God's power are being guarded through faith for a salvation ready to be revealed in the last time.' Some wonderful words there: imperishable, undefiled, and unfading. Stating those in the positive, our inheritance will last forever, will always be pure, and will be as beautiful in a million years as it is on day one. Then add to that the guarantee: it is already kept in heaven for us as Christians! Glorious!

Then there is controversial notion of rewards in heaven. This is a little tricky because we know we don't 'earn' heaven by what we do here. Only the blood of Christ qualifies us for eternal life. But Jesus himself teaches that there are rewards and treasure to be laid up in heaven by doing good in our early days. Giving a cup of cold water in Jesus's name (Matt. 10:41-42), loving one's neighbors (Luke 6:35), and surrendering one's relationships and good to the service of God (Matt. 19:28-29) are some of the things that lead to treasures in heaven. Indeed, we are to lay up treasures there rather than on earth (Matt. 6:20). This follows Jesus's teaching that we are not to do works to be seen by people, but in secret so that the Father who sees these secret deeds will reward us. This passage concludes with verse 21 that is particularly challenging, 'where your treasure is, there your heart will be also.'

Maybe the simplest way to explain this is that we do not merit reward for our works contractually – as though God might owe it to us. Rather, the abundant grace of God mandates that God will bless us for doing good despite this not being necessary. It is some-what like paying children for chores. As members of the family, they owe some work to the family. Yet parents, to encourage them to do well, may give an allowance for deeds done that should have been done anyway. How amazing is it that God would determine to bless sinners like us for rewarding loving deeds even when on our own we deserve hell!

These truths exhort us to consider where our treasure is after all. Facing death may expose that our treasure is more on earth than we might have thought. Grasping the greatness of the reward in heaven cannot only increase our eagerness for the gain of death, but to do more to 'invest' in the afterlife. More on this in the next chapter.

What Will We Do?

A final area worth considering is: what will we do in the afterlife? After all, eternity is a long time. While it is not plainly explained, the Bible gives us a few hints of what is to come. No activity is mentioned more than worship, as we will then 'worship the Lord in the splendor of holiness (Ps. 29:2), a theme echoed throughout Revelation. Revelation frequently makes mention of music, so that will be a large part of the worship in heaven. I often wonder how some Christians will do with this as they get bored with a mere hour-long worship service!

The Bible also suggests that we will serve the Lord as well, with a large part of this being the exertion of authority over the new earth (Rev. 7:14; Luke 19:17, 19; Matt. 25:22-23). Work is good as God does work (though I must say, He is incredibly efficient as He simply spoke the universe into existence). We all find types of work even here that bring us joy, so how would the work of the holy city be anything less than joyous?

While the Bible does not come right out and say it, there is certainly a sense that we will enjoy the fellowship of other believers, present and past (and future!). When speaking of the death of the great Martin Luther who had studied the saints of the Bible in detail, his successor Melanchthon envisioned, 'Now he embraces them and rejoices to hear them speak and to speak to them in turn. Now they hail him gladly as a companion, and thank God with him for having gathered and preserved the Church'[2]. This is representative of the long history of Christians holding to this idea. In times of grief we take comfort that we will see our loved ones again, but it is also exciting to anticipate meeting the believers who have gone before us!

It would also be difficult to imagine eternity without growth, and I am among those who also believe that we will learn and

---

2. Cited by Wilbur Smith in the book referenced earlier; p. 195.

mature in heaven. While we will instantly be without sin, for we could not be in God's presence otherwise, that does not imply we will not learn more about God and in the process come to love Him even more. Even with our new bodies, we won't know and understand God fully, but we will be ever drawing nearer to that ideal.

Finally, even though we'll be worshipping and serving and getting to know others, this will be a time of rest and refreshment. Our Sundays should hint at this (rooted in Exod. 20:8), with us laying aside the worries and concerns of the work-a-day world to focus on rest and fellowship with God and other believers. How much richer will the eternal Sabbath be, where even 'work' is restful (maybe something like a hobby is to us now). As I age, I feel a bit more tired. I value rest much more than I did when I was in my 20s. How sweet will it be to rest in the presence of my Savior. The peace of an infant in her mother's arms hints at the repose of knowing we are loved, protected, and ultimately secure.

These are absolutely delightful thoughts! Even in writing this, I wonder why I don't choose to spend more time considering it. As I think of heaven, my favorite restaurant or game or television program suddenly don't seem as satisfying. To die will be great gain!

If you are facing your own death, consider what awaits on the other side of Jordan. The suffering of these last days is like the pain of childbirth leading you to new life that will be more wonderful than the Promised Land was to Israel. If you are grieving the loss of someone special, or anticipating it, take comfort in the thought of what awaits your loved one in Christ.

Life in the holy city will be more wonderful than we can imagine, but that shouldn't keep us from spending more time thinking of our final destination!

8

To Live is Christ and to Die is Gain

For to me to live is Christ, and to die is gain.

Philippians 1:21

We may be more acquainted with the double negative: situations where we have to choose between two negative options. Pay a fine or go to jail. Pull a tooth or live in pain. Live with a conflict or confront a boss. We seem to notice these negatives all too readily. In contrast, Paul saw life and death as two positive outcomes. We touched on this in chapter 3 on Here and Hereafter. Now let's examine this a bit more closely from Paul's point of view.

We begin with Paul's discussion of why we defer to our brothers and sisters in Christ in Romans 14:7-9:

> *For none of us lives to himself, and none of us dies to himself. For if we live, we live to the Lord, and if we die, we die to the Lord. So then, whether we live or whether we die, we are the Lord's. For to this end Christ died and lived again, that he might be Lord both of the dead and of the living.*

We are not our own; we are the Lord's. That simple statement separates us dramatically from those in the world around us. Everyone is in it for himself or herself these days. We announce trivia on social media, we publicize ourselves with 'selfies' (there is actually a website that tracks the deaths of people who were killed trying to take dramatic 'selfies' of themselves!). Psychology promotes affirmation of one's self. More than we would like to think, preaching even panders to making people feel better about themselves and worship caters to personal taste.

Paul reminds us, in contrast, that we are not our own but we are bought with a price (1 Cor. 6:20; 7:23). We are no longer slaves to sin, but now are slaves to righteousness (Rom. 6:17-18). We have died with Christ and now live in Him (Rom. 6:8). We are radically different from those who live apart from Christ, for we have surrendered our lives to serve the One who died for us.

Facing death – whether our own or someone's near to us – can reveal how challenging it is to live in light of this biblical truth. In a selfie world, it is radically counter-cultural to live for someone else. In the context of Romans 14, our living and dying to others is the argument for treating others well when we disagree. All of this supports the simple statement that to live is Christ. It is not for ourselves as Christians. Considering the end of life can expose how we live for ourselves.

The Christian life is to be one of service to God, our Christian family, and the world around us. Paul rejoices in the Philippians despite being in prison. Why? Not because of his personal circumstances but because of how they were promoting the spread of the Gospel. He knows that so long as he lived, he would promote the cause of Christ

Our dread of death is natural since the Fall, but we worsen it when we lose sight of these powerful truths. We are so focused on our careers, our relationships, our goals and hopes, that we confuse our will with God's. If we are Christ's, it is up to Him when we are to be called home. We are, after all, His to dispose of as He sees best. This can be sad and painful, but if our faith is true, it is better for the person involved.

Here is the irony of physical versus spiritual death. Recall in the Garden of Eden that the same-day death God promised did not mean Adam and Eve stopped breathing. Rather, it meant that they were separated from a relationship with God. The clothes they donned showed they knew the intimate relationship they had known was over. They were spiritually 'dead' even as they breathed. This is sadly the case for most people today. They are breathing but dead in their trespasses and sin, alienated from a holy God. Their spiritual death will merely be completed by the physical death that awaits. I am afraid that I don't live as if I believe this. On the one hand, I sometimes expect more from unbelievers and forget that dead in sins is not a little bit alive. On the other hand, if I lived more consistently with this belief, I think I would be more active in praying for those without Christ and in spreading the good news of Jesus's death, burial, and resurrection (and His overcoming of death in the process).

For Christians the opposite holds. We have eternal life now because we have the new birth so famously spoken of in John 3:16. We enjoy fellowship with God every minute of every day, so long as we take advantage of this opportunity. We pray, praise, and rest in the knowledge that God never leaves or forsakes us (Heb. 13:5). In light of this new life, we live to God or, in Paul's words, to live is Christ. In gratitude for the forgiveness of sin that also brings a newness of spiritual life, we walk with and serve this loving God in all we do, think, and say. The shortcomings in our Christian lives betray how ungrateful we can be for our new life in Christ. I know I am guilty, and most likely you are, too.

In my part of the world, the death of a Christian is often called a 'homegoing' to reflect that the believer's home is with his or her Beloved. Physical death is not as daunting to those who are spiritually alive. We rejoice to have our souls come into the presence of our Saving God where we fellowship and worship in purer and more intimate ways than we even imagined on earth. The death of a Christian disrupts earthly relationships (albeit with hope for these to be renewed in the future), but only draws us closer into relationship with God Himself as we are freed of these sinful bodies.

Part of the sadness of the death of loved ones is the loss of relationship it brings to us personally. We are grateful to think that they share in the glory of God, being freed from the sin and suffering that are so much a part of the world we live in. Yet, we grieve the broken relationship their parting brings to us. Before sin entered the world, God declared that it is not good for man to be alone (Gen. 2:18). If that were true prior to sin, we infer that it will be after sin has entered the world. Human relationships are vital to all of us, be they family, church, friends, or colleagues. So we do grieve when these relationships are lost to us – but not as those who have no hope.

To live is indeed Christ, and when death draws near, whether to us or a loved one, it reminds us of the importance of redeeming our time on earth (Eph. 5:16) for the days are indeed evil. Thoughts of death can spur us to live our lives more heartily in the light of eternal realities.

But to die is also gain. Death of those who die in Christ is a mixed blessing – we rejoice that they now more fully enter into relationship with God while we mourn our separation from them. For us as individuals, death is gain for we finally enjoy complete freedom from sin, opening the door to perfect, sweet fellowship with our Lord and Savior. May God grant us grace to live out these inspired words in our own lives, no matter what our circumstances and challenges!

9

Blessed are Those
Who Mourn

*Blessed are those who mourn, for
they will be comforted.*

MATTHEW 5:4

As we draw our first section of reflections to a close, a brief review may be in order. We may have seemed to contradict ourselves as we've gone along. We began by looking at how modern culture represses the thought of death and has done its best to move death out of public view. But then we considered the biblical teachings on the subject of death and resurrection, and found not only hope for the future, but a charge to live our remaining lives on earth in radical obedience to God because of the hope of eternal life with Him. While culture may be guilty of repressing death, the Christian message can be wrongly seen as minimizing death into 'no big deal' because of the hope of the resurrection.

In this chapter we are reminded of the balance. While death is real, and so is resurrection, death still is a challenge for those facing it and those walking through dying with a loved one. Christians, both leaders and lay persons, are often guilty of taking the truths of Scripture and turning them into cold, unfeeling platitudes that bring little comfort. Comfort is, after all, unnecessary if there is no pain and suffering. The comforts of Christian fellowship and the Christian message are not meant to gloss over the profound sorrow that death brings. Jesus did not.

Jesus brings up mourning in the second of the Beatitudes, cited at the beginning of this chapter. Kingdom people are mourners, and they will be comforted. While certainly a major aspect of this is mourning for our sinfulness, it leaves room for mourning death, the consequence of sin, as well. Part of the denial of death we discussed earlier is the denial of mourning.[1] Our culture keeps us entertained every waking moment, with television, Internet, and smart phones giving us a video to watch or a game to play so that every free moment can be spent having fun. Even as I write, the Internet calls should I tire for a moment of the concentration required to write. This omnipresent entertainment effectively separates us from the experience of our emotions, and so we come to avoid unpleasant feelings at all costs. This is something new to our generation, as people were not so insulated for most of history.

We can, then, deny the sorrow of death even as we try to deny its very existence. Grief is often made private – as though it is an embarrassment to mourn the death of a loved one, or even to commemorate it with black clothes or other signs of mourning. We allow the family several days to welcome the comfort of friends and families, hold a funeral service, and then lay the body of the loved one to rest. We all go home, then, often leaving the bereaved to continue their grief in private – if not implicitly sending them the message that the grieving is over and they should get back to normal. Part of this may come from the way our news comes to us in this day and age. If there is a tragedy, news channels give it 24-hour coverage for a while, but soon it disappears into the background. The recovery of a city hit by an earthquake or the mourning of families who lost loved ones in a mass shooting don't make headlines after the event itself.

Grieving after the death of a loved one really gets started after the funeral. The busyness of making arrangements, traveling, and interacting with those who come to comfort can keep a person so busy that grief is pushed to the background. Then everyone goes

---

1. Some of the major points of this chapter are adapted from Allen Verhey, *The Christian Art of Dying: Learning from Jesus* (Grand Rapids, MI: Eerdmans), 2011.

home, and the family is often left to return to a life that is no longer the same. It is in these days, weeks, and months that comfort may be most desperately needed.

Why do we do this? We are busy with our own lives, of course, yet Christians say we value ministry to those who suffer. Partly we may feel awkward, not knowing what to say so we don't say anything. I recall in my own life this insight when I finally got it: being with a mourner is about being there, not saying some magic words that fix everything. Many of us instinctively avoid discomfort, and so we may dodge the uncertainties that come with spending time with a grieving friend or church member. Even pastors and church leaders may do well prayerfully to reflect on their reasoning for not following up much with grieving parishioners.

Mourning calls for comforting, and that requires companionship, being with the mourner. We need to take the time to visit the funeral home or go to the wake. We can do things like take food to the family, but most important is simply to be there – and 'there' may be after the formal funeral process.

We need not come bearing trite phrases that may have an element of truth, but miss the realities. Perhaps we come with comments like 'Don't be so sad; she is with Jesus now.' Telling people not to feel sad is actually quite unsympathetic. Think about it: can you turn off an emotion when someone simply tells you to? Not likely – and even less likely when that emotion is as profound as grief. It is important to understand that even though there is the positive side, there is still the loss. A mother can be very happy to see her daughter marry, yet grieve the change this brings in their relationship. We can also be grateful that a loved one is no longer suffering and is with Jesus, but we still will miss them and lament the changes in our life that ensue.

Possibly the worst comforters ever were those who came to be with Job. We cannot imagine the loss he experienced – riches, family, and health all taken suddenly. Here come his 'friends' with words that would exacerbate the problem. Verhey says its well:

> *The problem they said was not that they had no answers for Job, but that they thought they had them all. They claimed to know too*

much and to know it too clearly. They thought they needed to be the defense attorneys for God, but they ended up as prosecutors of Job. (p. 341)

We can be like that, especially if we come in pastoral roles. We want to make the person feel better, but if we look more closely, it may be that we are uncomfortable with the pain or the awkwardness of the situation. It is not likely that anything we say will make the pain go away. That is not the goal anyway. It is to be with the person and ease the suffering, not to make it go away. We must resist the temptation to avoid going to be with the mourner because of the awkwardness of not knowing what to say, but also we should not offer trite advice and 'comfort' for the same reason.

We primarily are just to be with the one who mourns. If it was not good for man to be alone in Eden (Genesis 2:18), why would it be good when a man (or woman) is in mourning? There are things not to say, and things maybe to say. There is hope in Christ, but sadness in death. We get through loss only because of the grace of God, yet the presence of others can be a primary means by which grace comes to the mourner.

In the sections that follow we will be more specific and practical about preparing for, going through, and moving on after death. We will be honest and straightforward, knowing that death is an enemy, but a defeated one. We will strive together to bring glory to God in how we mourn as we face our own death and the deaths of loved ones. May the God of all comfort teach us how we may be of comfort to one another, even as we know we are blessed when we mourn.

Part II

As a Loved One is Dying

❧❧

Introduction

Death can come suddenly or after an agonizing, lengthy illness. The former gives no time to prepare for the loss. In many cases, though, loved ones and fellow church members have opportunity to share in the final journey. This section is intended for those who walk with someone who is likely to die before very long. Others may benefit from it, for most all of us will join in such a journey at some point in our lives. Even those who are dying might benefit from this section in order to have a greater appreciation of the experience of those around them.

This is a trying time. We struggle hoping the loved one lives, yet brace ourselves for death. We may face decisions about care and whether the loved one should be at home or in a medical facility. We may grow weary and sad as we struggle through each day. I pray the pages ahead offer some support, direction, and consolation as you pass through these dark waters.

10

The Role of Church Leadership in Caring for the Dying

Even though I walk through the valley
of the shadow of death,
I will fear no evil, for you are with me

PSALM 23:4a

How fitting that we begin this section of our reflections on the same note with which we finished our last: companionship in the face of death. In the verse above the Psalmist takes comfort in knowing that God is with him even when death is near. Indeed, God is with all of His children as we encounter death for 'precious in the sight of the LORD is the death of his saints' (Ps. 116:15). Often, however, God's presence is made more manifest by the presence and comfort of the leaders of the church. We begin this section with some thoughts of the ways pastors and other church leaders can bring comfort and clarity into the lives of the dying ones under their care, and to their families.

A surprising model for this ministry for all who come to comfort the dying is Simon of Cyrene (e.g., Matt. 27:32) who was conscripted into carrying the cross of Christ as Jesus was being led to His death. We, too, will be called upon to intercede and bear the burden of others on the road to their passing into glory. We will need to point them to the abundance of God's grace. What are

65

some of the ways spiritual leaders can assist those who are dying and those who love them?

First, we can educate those in our churches about dying, death, the resurrection, and the afterlife. In our denial of death, these topics are not preached on very often. Our churches may play to the tastes of younger people so much that we do not speak much of death and the needs of aging members of congregations (and I'm afraid many independent congregations that are trying to reach younger generations may not have many older adults in them).

Historically, the church celebrated the death of saints in church history, reminding congregations of those who have gone before. Protestants may over-react to Catholic prayers to the saints by neglecting to even tell the stories of those who have passed the faith along since biblical times. We do well to be reminded of the great cloud of witnesses (Heb. 12:1) in the Bible and since. Our connectedness to our spiritual family reminds us of death and the glory after it. Churches might even commemorate the deaths of members of their local bodies from time to time. Some rural churches where my mother grew up have an annual 'decoration' of the graves in the cemeteries near the church to celebrate the lives of those gone before and to maintain the bonds of family who remain.

Consider offering occasional sermons or classes that teach about the nature of death, the relation of body and soul, and the life hereafter. Many Christians are uneducated and thus fear death partly out of ignorance. No, this isn't a great headline-catching sermon topic, but it is part of feeding the flock. Some churches offer grief workshops and this is commendable, but more is needed prior to the loss. Our older members won't be here indefinitely, and death even strikes younger people at times. It is best for church leadership to prepare their people to cope with death, be it their own or others in the congregation. Such classes could help equip the congregation on how to care for the dying within the church and in the surrounding community as well. Yes, even children can be involved by making crafts or performing service to those who are dying and the families caring for them.

Proactive education helps the church avoid the denial of death so rampant in our culture. We cannot become so eager to accommodate modern tastes that we fail to serve the sheep in our flocks. Death is sad, but it is inevitable until Jesus returns.

Pastoral prayers can help 'cue' memory of deceased saints and promote awareness of the reality of death. Pray for families who have lost loved ones on the anniversaries of their deaths. Other men and women in the church might bring a meal or send a card (or even an email) to families long after the funeral is over. As we have seen, mourning doesn't end when the funeral is over, and we need to minister to this ongoing grief actively in our churches.

Beyond education and building awareness, there are numerous ways church leaders can comfort families facing death of a loved one. First, pray carefully. While certainly there is warrant in Scripture to pray for healing and restoration, we must concede that God eventually calls all of us home. As we note in several places, there is a tendency, partly due to the medicalization of death, that we expect everyone to get well every time. Where medicine may fail, we believe God can make it happen. Again, this is wonderful as far as it goes. But there is a point where we must acknowledge that, until the Lord returns, we all die at some point. I confess I lack the wisdom to say when one stops praying for healing and begins praying for death – I am sure it varies with each situation. There may also be reason to pray simultaneously for healing and to prepare the person for a good death.

In my mind, the central idea is not to see death as a defeat as the medical model would have it. Death is inevitable, and when it seems fairly certain that a person is dying, Christian leaders may want to work with that person and his or her family to get the closure and comfort that comes from admitting death is near and preparing for it. After all, there is no Easter without Good Friday, and we will not be raised without going through death first.

This can be accomplished by bringing up the topic and asking if the person and family have given it much thought. One may have to take care not to come across as lacking faith for healing, but as embracing faith in the goodness of God to accomplish

His purposes – even if they include the death of the loved one in question. This is definitely a tricky call, but we must help our brothers and sisters see that God is sovereign, even over life and death. If He were not, then we would be without hope.

Breaching the topic gives the leader opportunity to let the dying person and family members begin the grieving process and go through the processes we will be describing in subsequent chapters. It might open the door to discuss difficult things with family members such as advance directives should extreme medical procedures be considered, or to begin to discuss where the family and individual wants the death to occur: home or hospital. The leader may get permission to invite the church to comfort the family and walk through these last days with the individual and his or her family.

It is vital to avoid those clichés that easily come in these times, such as 'he will be in a better place' or 'she will be in heaven with Aunt Martha.' The comfort of the hope of eternal life needs to sit atop a powerful empathy with the grief of the person who is dying and the family. Don't be in too big of a rush to make it all better. Death is not easily glossed over. Be with the family and let your words be few.

A strength of many churches is that they dispatch a minister or other leader to be with the dying brother or sister in Christ in the final hours. Strive to be present to the family as much as they desire for the days and weeks leading up to this. See if the family would want a group of church members to come and be with and pray for them. Does your church offer a way to bring communion to the bed of the dying person so that he or she may partake a last time prior to going to be with God? Be available to help fill in gaps in the family's theological understanding of death and dying.

And we would not forget the challenge of being with a person who does not profess Christ. Like the thief on the cross, this may be the moment God uses to bring salvation. Pray for and witness to the person while not trying to replace the work of the Holy Spirit through pressure. Comfort believing family members even as together you wrestle with the mystery of the ways of God.

While being with those who are faced with the death of a loved one may be one of the single hardest tasks for pastors and church leaders, it is one of the most profound opportunities to minister grace to our brothers and sisters. Let us all pray for wisdom for those who step into the role of Simon of Cyrene.

11

Hoping for Life or Preparing for Death?

I ask you neither for health nor for sickness,
for life nor for death,
but that You may dispose my health and my sickness,
my life and my death
for Your glory ...
You alone know what is expedient for me,
You are the sovereign master;
Do with me according to Your will.
Give to me or take away from me,
Only conform my will to yours.

PRAYER OF BLAISE PASCAL[1]

The instinct to stay alive is one of the most powerful ones we have. Consider that pretty much any fear you might have is in some way related to protecting yourself and staying alive. Fear of heights? Of course falling is dangerous. Fear of germs? They can make you sick and even bring death in some circumstances. We see drivers as 'crazy' when they drive in ways that endanger themselves and others. I am sure you get the point. We instinctively don't want to die. We don't even have to think about it in most cases: we act to protect ourselves – and those we love.

---

1. From *Thoughts, Prayers and Minor Works of Blaise Pascal*, p. 377. At https://archive.org/details/thoughtslettersm028185mbp last accessed 2/14/2017.

Why would this not hold true when we are aware that we are facing death itself? We may fear not only dying, but what death will be like. We, like Paul, may be torn between life and death, living on to serve God, or being with him. We will have the same conflict about those we love as we walk with them through the valley of the shadow of death.

So how, then, to pray? Is it faithless to resolve ourselves to the death of a loved one? We recall how desperately David prayed for his illegitimate child by Bathsheba: 'David therefore sought God on behalf of the child. And David fasted and went in and lay all night on the ground' (2 Sam. 12:16). If you follow the account, he arose once the child died. Plainly, he was not content simply to commit the fate of his child to God. I find no warrant in Scripture not to pray for those who are dying.

Conversely, if dying is gain, why are we so persistent in insisting that God not take those we love? If the afterlife is so wonderful, why would we long so for our loved ones to continue in this woeful earthly existence? How wonderful it will be to be where there is no sin and suffering and every tear is wiped from our eyes (Rev. 7:17)! Why would we ever prefer this world to that? Or why would we implore God to leave a loved one here rather than enter that bliss?

Our instinct to live is one explanation, and our fear of the unknown is another. In the end, it is more comfortable to the individual to keep things as they are, for at least the current situation is familiar. David may have had mixed motives in his prayer as he was aware that he might bear responsibility for the death of his child conceived in adultery and murder.

How do Christians decide what to do: hope for life or prepare for death? We've seen in this book earlier how there is a strong cultural impulse toward denying death and letting it sneak up on us. We may pray so hard for recovery of a loved one that we may view his or her death as a failure of not praying hard enough or trusting God enough. Death is tragic already without adding some sense of guilt or responsibility to it.

But it may seem cold to feel like you are giving up and accepting death as inevitable – not to mention a bit unnatural. It feels awkward to say that you are praying for someone to have a good death. While psychologically it may help to brace us if we 'hope for the best and prepare for the worst', we can also feel guilty for giving up hope too soon.

To consider a solution, let us back up a bit for some perspective. If we take seriously our faith and genuinely seek to honor God with our lives and to see Him honored in the lives of those we love, we can see things a little differently. To illustrate this, let me borrow from the great early church father, Augustine,[2] who boils this down to the peace of those who serve God. What brings us peace in this present world? That a man 'submit himself to God, his body to his soul, and his vices, even when they rebel, to his reason … and that he beg from God grace to do his duty.' The central thought here is submission. If we are not our own because we were bought with a price (1 Cor. 6:20), and are slaves to righteousness (Rom. 6:19), we understand that our responsibility is submission to our benevolent Master. We are at His disposal, as troops under a general. Troops don't ask not to be sent to battle or seek the safest deployment, but ask only to be used to further the cause of the One to whom they are committed.

This leads us to the conclusion that we may struggle against the will of God when we try to dictate what He should do. I believe we pray for those who are ill and seem to be dying, yet we do so in the spirit of Jesus who prayed in the Garden of Gethsemane, 'My Father, if it be possible, let this cup pass from me; nevertheless, not as I will, but as you will' (Matt. 26:39). If we are His, we will be aware of what we want in ourselves and even ask for it, but be ready to submit to the wisdom of the almighty and all-wise God.

After all, the option of death is not as grievous as we might think. Augustine goes on (in the same chapter) to describe the final peace that awaits the follower of Christ:

> Our nature shall enjoy a sound immortality and incorruption, and shall have no more vices, and we shall experience no resistance

---

2. Drawn from his *City of God*, Book 19, Chapter 27.

either from ourselves or from others, it will not be necessary that reason should rule vices that no longer exist, but God shall rule the man, and the soul shall rule the body, with a sweetness and facility suitable to the felicity of a life which is done with bondage.

The peace of being freed from the bondages of sinful bodies and a sinful world will bring peace that we cannot imagine. Augustine's words should give new meaning to the tired cliché, 'Rest in peace'. Oh, what rest! Oh, what peace!

In short, we cannot 'lose'. If God grants the loved one life, then he or she is free to submit and serve God until the day comes when God calls that person home. Should God take this person, we know that rest and peace follow, provided by a God who loves this person more than we possibly could.

So should we pray for hope or prepare for death? Jump ahead some 1,200 years from Augustine to Blaise Pascal, who offered the prayer shown at the beginning of this chapter. It reflects an attitude that I call divine indifference. So long as God is glorified, as those who submit to God, we will accept whichever God deems. It is a prayer that reflects Jesus's words in the Garden. We don't know whether living or dying is best at any given moment. Paul's 'to live is Christ and to die is gain' is followed in the next verse by words that reflect our point: 'Yet which I shall choose I cannot tell' (Phil. 1:22).

Let me conclude by being more precise. If you have a loved one who is ill, by all means, pray that God will preserve him or her – if it is indeed His will. But also prepare yourself and others around that person should God's will be to translate the loved one into eternal peace and rest. Reconcile yourself to this possibility as God's will, even if it is a bitter providence. As Augustine noted, submit yourself to God and to what He has for you and for the loved one. Rejoice if the person recovers, but rejoice also if God ends his or her suffering forever! In the meantime, make any necessary preparations should the person die, if you have responsibilities for doing so. If you are a parent and the person who is ill is *your* parent or other close relative, alert your children to the possibilities unless they are very young (say, under five years). If you are a church leader, help the family find a place closer to this 'divine indifference'. If a hospital requests end-of-life arrangements be made, then make them. Don't live in denial of the possibility of death.

Do not concede that the person will die, either. Pray for recovery, and maintain hope that God indeed can make that happen. But in so doing do not see death, should it come, as a defeat. Some options are more painful than others, but there are no bad outcomes to those who are in Christ.

❧ PRAYER ❧

God, grant us grace to submit ourselves to your will,
even as we are mindful that we are but dust and
wrestle with the reality of death.

12

Being With and Caring for the Dying

The Spirit of the Lord GOD is upon me,
because the LORD has anointed me
... to comfort all who mourn

ISAIAH 61:1-2

They say every snowflake is unique, and I believe the same might be said about every death. They range from startlingly sudden deaths to lives that linger for months and even years only because of medical assistance. Some are painless; others are wracked with pain. Some are peaceful; others are tumultuous. To write about how to be with one who is dying is a challenge, for I have no idea what your situation is like now, or how it will end. I will offer some thoughts on the topic, well aware that not all will apply to your situation and that there will be uniquenesses you face that I do not cover.

We have discussed the tension between hoping for life and preparing for death. For many, the current chapter will be rather irrelevant for death came to your loved one suddenly and there was little or no time to prepare yourself or walk through the process with the deceased. There are intermediate situations where one is ill and it seems he or she may have a while before death comes, then the illness takes a sudden turn for the worse. As we noted, each story is unique. I invite the reader to choose from what follows to suit his or her individual situation, even as the focus is on a death that is gradual.

When a loved one is ill the prognosis may suggest a need to begin preparing for death. There may be legal and financial arrangements to be made, but we are focusing more on the spiritual and emotional dimensions of the process. Things may reach the point where death seems fairly inevitable. If you are walking through the dying phase of a loved one's life, you may need to reach a point of acceptance that this person will not survive the illness or injury. It is impossible to say for the individual case when one should come to accept the upcoming death, but there may be harm in denying this too long.

Dying well involves gaining closure with people and God, and a caregiver that is in denial can deprive the dying person of this opportunity if he or she is not realistic about what is about to happen. Sometimes caregivers will accept the upcoming death first; other times the dying person will come to terms with it first. But a good death is aided by all parties conceding the certainty of what is to come. If you as caregiver reach this first, you will need to be gentle in dealing with the dying person if he or she is struggling to come to terms with impending death.

Family members may team up to make critical decisions such as the setting for the beloved's last days: hospital, home, skilled care facility, or some place else? Another decision may be whether care will be given by family or professionals, or whether hospice care is used and to what extent. The wisdom and experience of hospice medical staff may be a great resource for maximizing the comfort of the person who is dying. Websites such as dyingmatters.org offer helpful information, and becoming educated about the matters meriting attention prior to and after death is a valuable ministry to your loved one.

We will focus, though, on what you as caregiver (family member, church member, spiritual leader, or simply friend) can do to be with and care for this special one during this final chapter of earthly life.

When God first made man, it was not good that he be alone, so as we noted earlier, it seems quite reasonable that it is not good for the dying person to be alone. This is hard for it is uncomfortable. Not only is the loved one going through stormy emotions, but you are likely dealing with the same. We have a proclivity to avoid uncomfortable feelings, but this is not the time for that.

You may not have words to say or great wisdom to offer, but you offer a most critical commodity: your presence and attention. We have an aged dog in our home who is in poor health and we await his death any day. Yet even this animal will walk over just to stand by us as he is apparently in pain and great discomfort. Why would human beings not value the same? And the dog obviously is not soliciting words of wisdom, but the comfort of being near his master.

Being present with the dying one is a sacred honor. You may seek occasion to help the person walk through some of the 'final business' of making peace with God and family as described in Part III of this book. Your gentle nudge may make the difference in the person dying at peace or in the way other loved ones gain closure in the relationship with the individual. You may facilitate a review of the person's life, for reflecting on one's story is a meaningful way to prepare for the final chapter. You will need to be sensitive to the one you care for and not push things he or she is not ready for, yet your wise questions about favorite memories, happy times, and the words of Scripture may spur the person to healthy preparation for death.

While words may be few, or maybe unnecessary at all if the person is incoherent or deaf, your presence may be felt, even if not seen or heard. Meaningful gazes directed toward the person can also communicate love and concern. Even performing the unpleasant rituals of cleaning bedpans or sheets, or sponging the person down show tender affection. Maybe more than words or just being attentive, touch is a powerful comforter. Did you know simply holding hands can decrease blood pressure? Doing that or gently rubbing a forearm can be a ministry of comfort to the one who is dying. Spouses or closer relatives might gently touch the cheek or kiss the forehead. Whatever is suitable, touch is comforting in most cases (the exception being if it causes physical pain).

Many assert that hearing is the last sense to shut down when one is dying. Often a person that appears otherwise unresponsive can recognize a voice and words. Just the familiarity of the voice of someone dear can minister to the person. Simple phrases such as 'I'm here with you' are all that need be said, but a little more on this in a moment.

As you are with the dying person, look for ways that God issues special grace. The first Christian martyr, Stephen, just before he was fatally pelted with rocks, looked into heaven and saw Jesus at the right hand of God (Acts 7:55-56). It is not uncommon for God to minister to the dying and those with them in special ways as the end draws near. As you care for the one you love, be alert to the possibility that grace will show up in surprising ways: a look of peace or smile on the person's face, a moment of coherence to speak last words to a loved one. I think we overlook these sometimes because in our grief we miss the gentle stirrings of the One who walks with us through the valley of the shadow of death.

Let us close this chapter with a few reflections on ways to care for the person when we are with him or her. One of the most important services you might offer is to advocate for the best care possible. Many health providers are busy and distracted, and may not serve the dying as well as they might. You might be the one to have hospice called so that specialists are available. You might see that a nurse can come to the home, or prescriptions are filled, or the most comfortable bedding is offered. Again, the multitude of variety in dying means that your needs will be unique, but regardless, be a voice for the dying person and advocate. Facilitate communication and coordination of care with the medical and other professional staff. You may also coordinate with ministers at your church to arrange for communion to be brought to the loved one, giving opportunity to participate in this means of grace and all of its significance.

In speaking to the dying person, you may help him or her express concerns and fears. A listening ear is all that is required, not the magic words to fix things. Be a person that shows the dying person that you accept their impending death and are not reluctant to let the person talk frankly to you about it. Help the person reflect on the joys of the afterlife that await, and to consider the value his or her life had for God's kingdom in general and the family in particular. We mentioned above some other ways you can promote meaningful conversation in these last days. You may also help the person meditate through some of the material in this book, particularly the section directed to those who are dying.

Even if you observe a decline in rationality and coherence, the failing brain enjoys familiar things, and for the Christian, the soul also is comforted by familiar Scriptures and songs. Sing quietly to the person, or play recordings of familiar hymns and Christian songs. Simple phrases repeated frequently offer consolation. An ancient tradition is the saying of the Jesus prayer, 'Lord Jesus Christ, have mercy on me a sinner.' For the dying person, simply repeating 'Lord have mercy' is a gracious service. Remember: hearing continues when other senses seem to be shut down.

Pray with and for the person … not desperate prayers for healing at this point, but prayers of hope and anticipation of the glory that awaits. The sadness is bittersweet, for it is mixed with hope and an end to suffering.

Finally, take care of yourself. Don't be super-spiritual and suggest you can do it all. Receive help from your church, family, and friends. If you need it or you need relief for a while, ask for it. You will care better if you take care of yourself. This is one of the most emotionally draining things you will ever do. God will be with you, but he will also use the comfort and support of His people to walk you through this dark hour.

❧ PRAYER ❦

Loving and gracious God, pour out grace on those
who are ill and dying, but also we ask special
mercies for those who serve You by serving those
who die. May the presence of Your Comforter be
obvious as they walk through the valley.

13

Praying and Praising Through the Process

For if we live, we live to the Lord, and if we die, we die to the Lord. So then, whether we live or whether we die, we are the Lord's. For to this end Christ died and lived again, that he might be Lord both of the dead and of the living.

ROMANS 14:8-9

Christians are praying people. The Bible teaches us so to do, and prayer has been an anchor of Christian worship and practice throughout history. It is obviously a resource that will be called upon in ministering to the dying and those close to the patient.[1] Let us, then, take a little time to think through what such prayer might be like – and even consider the praise that might accompany it.

First, recall that we saw there is room to continue to pray for restoration of the sick loved one, even after we reach a point of accepting that death is the most likely ending to the present illness. I would not overlook the prayer for healing, though this is so commonly practiced that we need not elaborate on it here. But such intercession for the ill is to be tempered by the need to prepare for death when it appears inevitable. While God can always break

---

1. In case some are troubled when I use the term 'patient', I wish to clarify that I use it in its historic meaning: a person who is patient under affliction. Medicalization usurps the term from this rich ancient meaning, and leaves us seeing it as simply one seeking medical help.

through in miraculous ways, death should not be taken as a failure of healing prayer, but as God's sovereign will for what is best. The dying person does not need to finish his or her days feeling that death itself is letting down loved ones.

The mixed feelings of sadness and hope that we feel when a child of God dies are far less mixed when we fear the dying person is not a Christian. While we do not understand fully, we know that none other than 'gentle Jesus' spoke more of hell than of heaven. Many of us live as though this is not true anyway, acting as though hurting someone's feelings by sharing the Gospel is a greater sin than blithely letting them slip into hell. The thief on the cross gives great hope for deathbed conversions, and all who believe in Christ should pray – and fast – for the salvation of those outside of Christ who are dying. This is, of course, a reminder that we have room to grow in praying for the lost when they are healthy also.

With these thoughts in the background, we will review some approaches to prayer for the dying and those near them. These prayers may be offered for or even with the dying person. These can also be easily adapted to lift up the family and loved ones, and be said for and with them. Rather than give specific prayers, I offer some ideas that can be modified for use in the particular context you are dealing with.

Praise God

One of the important ways to pray in difficult times is to praise God. Praising God also serves to remind us – and the patient – of important truths of God. The passage from Romans above is a wonderful example, affording a reminder of God's sovereignty over life and death. We can adapt these words to offer thanks to God for His wonderful wisdom and power in giving or taking life. We can rejoice that the loved one is the Lord's, whether life or death lies in the days ahead. This is a pivot for all prayer for the dying, it seems to me, as we are comforted by knowing that nothing can separate our loved one from the Lord (Rom. 8:35-39).

A passage that is a particularly rich vein of gold for our prayers is 1 Peter 1:3-9:

> *Blessed be the God and Father of our Lord Jesus Christ! According to his great mercy, he has caused us to be born again to a living hope through the resurrection of Jesus Christ from the dead, to an inheritance that is imperishable, undefiled, and unfading, kept in heaven for you, who by God's power are being guarded through faith for a salvation ready to be revealed in the last time. In this you rejoice, though now for a little while, if necessary, you have been grieved by various trials, so that the tested genuineness of your faith—more precious than gold that perishes though it is tested by fire—may be found to result in praise and glory and honor at the revelation of Jesus Christ. Though you have not seen him, you love him. Though you do not now see him, you believe in him and rejoice with joy that is inexpressible and filled with glory, obtaining the outcome of your faith, the salvation of your souls.*

It is a challenge just to find a starting point for prayer and praise based on this text. But we are to join the apostle in praise to God for the resurrection of Jesus and for the living hope that we have because of it. This is why we have great hope for the patient, even as we anticipate his or her death. We pray that our loved one can catch a clearer image of what awaits in heaven. We offer prayer specifically that this person will be comforted to know that ahead is an inheritance that is not and never will be defiled nor fading. We can pray, too, that the patient's faith in what lies ahead be zealously guarded and strengthened by the God who has made this inheritance available through Christ. We pray that the current trials of suffering will be valued as a preparation for the praise and glory that awaits, seeking God's grace for faith to see this wonderful hope even while the loved one cannot yet see it. This may be the focal idea: prayer that God will grant grace and faith to the patient to find hope and comfort in the awareness of the wonder that lies ahead. Here prayer and praise blend as we seek the Comforter Himself to enhance our hope and faith, whether we are the one dying or the Simon of Cyrene walking through the valley with him or her.

Do Not Be Afraid

The most common command in all of Scripture is some form of 'do not be afraid'. The weakness of our faith means that most of us will experience fear as we go through the process of dying. Some may misunderstand the command as though it was intended to scold us for our lack of faith. I believe it is spoken in comfort when you look at the context in which it occurs most often. Note, for example, that this command is frequent when God's people in the Bible encounter angels. Being so tied to our physical realities, it is quite a shock when the spiritual breaks in on us. This seems to capture what happens at death when we leave the physical for a time to enter the spiritual until the resurrection of our bodies. Prayer that the patient will not be afraid seems wise – and one that is applicable clearly to those who walk with him or her.

Comfort

Similarly, those who mourn are promised the blessing of comfort according to Jesus (Matt. 5:4). Jesus also promised the Holy Spirit will serve as Helper or Comforter (John 15:26). Is there doubt that God will keep His promises? Sometimes we pray as if He won't. For example, a common prayer in my circles is to ask God to 'be with' whomever we are praying for. There is an irony in that: since God is everywhere and promised never to leave nor forsake us, how would he *not* be with that person? God has promised, so doesn't need a reminder. Rather, the issue, it seems to me, is that we walk in light of that truth and don't wander into thinking and acting as if this weren't true. We might ask, then, that God overcome the distractions, fear, and earthly-mindedness and maybe even sin that hinder enjoyment of His presence.

We pray then that our loved one will know deeply the comfort of God that He has promised, with neither pain and suffering nor human weakness blinding our patient to the love and grace of God. This may include a prayer that the person will know more than ever the presence of the Good Shepherd who is walking with him or her through the valley of the shadow of death (Ps. 23:4), and that the sting of death (1 Cor. 15:55) has been defeated by the One who is shepherding this loved one home. Pray, too, that the person be protected from the insidious assaults of Satan who would cause doubt and fear during this most difficult chapter of life.

Eternal Hope

Along with comfort, and similar to what we saw in 1 Peter, we pray for the patient to know the hope that comes with the reality of the resurrection. This is the climax of Paul's long discussion of the resurrection in 1 Corinthians 15, particularly in verses 54-57. We pray for comfort as the patient suffers, says good-bye to loved ones, and seeks peace for the life story that is now ending. But we add to this the great hope we have in Christ's resurrection and His gracious allowing us to share in it. Pray that all those around the patient, too, will greet death with this hope that shines even in a cloudy sky.

Grace

Finally, pray that the patient and all that are affected will find grace to surrender to God's wisdom and yield the life of the loved one into the hands of God. Jesus Himself used the words of Psalm 31:5a, 'Into your hand I commit my spirit', signifying a letting go of this life and a final act of submission and self-denial. The first martyr, Stephen, used similar words as he faced death, praying, 'Lord Jesus, receive my spirit' (Acts 7:59). As death approaches, there is great comfort in knowing that as we lose control over our bodies, the spirit is received into the powerful yet gentle hands of our risen Savior. This is a beautiful way to pray at the end of life as we formally hand over the loved one to our Lord, knowing the peace that comes in the assurance that the patient need be patient no longer, but is to receive the promised blessing of God. Pray, too, that those near the loved one will find grace to let go of efforts to control the fate of the patient and surrender their own wills to God as did Jesus and Stephen.

❧ PRAYER ❦

Lord Jesus, we are weak and struggle to grasp all You have
done for us – particularly as we face the end of life. Grant
us grace to know with Paul in Romans 8:38-39:

For I am sure that neither *death nor life*, nor angels
nor rulers, nor things present nor things to come,
nor powers, nor height nor depth, nor anything else
in all creation, will be able to separate us from the
love of God in Christ Jesus our Lord.
(*italics mine*)

14

The Role of the Christian Community in Care and Comfort

And the King will answer them, 'Truly, I say to you, as you did it to one of the least of these my brothers, you did it to me.'

MATTHEW 25:40

The verse above ends Jesus's discussion of what will matter at the final judgment. Financially prosperous careers or ministries, best-selling books or albums, large houses, or any other forms of fame and fortune are not what ultimately matters. Rather, caring for those in need is the key, particularly when the caring isn't glamorous. Though those who sit in vigil over a dying loved one or grieve one recently deceased are not mentioned explicitly in the text, I do not see it as a stretch at all to see service to these dear ones as fulfilling the mission Jesus has for His people to care for the 'least of these' brothers of his – and ours.

Yet as we noted earlier, the Christian community has in large part handed over the care of the dying person to the medical community and easily accommodates to a contemporary culture that hides death from view as much as possible. Even as Christians, we may hide death by using language which masks the reality, calling it 'passing away' or 'crossing Jordan' rather than calling death by its name. It seems warranted, then, to take one chapter here to consider how the family of Christ can embrace those near to those who are dying or recently deceased.

Let us begin with a few comments on how the church and Christians within it are doing in caring for the dying. We are often good at praying, something we've discussed earlier. We are good at bringing food for the family just after a death (at least that is a tradition in my corner of the world). We may send cards or flowers. We do better when the family is close to us.

But we have some weaknesses, too, I'm afraid. Often the business of dealing with those who are dying is attended to by the older persons in the congregation who are more sensitive to the reality of death. We may visit the family just after the funeral, but aren't as consistent in caring for those who keep vigil over a chronically ill family member or after the funeral is over. Age segregation in our churches may keep younger folks from awareness of the process. The older persons who die are often homebound and not as well known to newer, younger members of the congregation. This makes it all too easy to pass along the societal denial of death. Then there is the overall discomfort and awkwardness of being around those who are struggling with anxiety about the fate of a loved one or grief at having lost someone special. As we've noted, our responses are often trained by news media that makes a big deal of an event for a couple of days, then discarding the event for something new. We don't do as well with sustained care, yet that is what is needed in the case of chronic illness and death.

The role of the church in this is to bear one another's burdens (Gal. 6:2) and to bring all of the Spirit's gifts (1 Cor. 12:4-11) to bear for one another. This requires sacrifice and – something that we have become allergic to in our day – discomfort. It is a strange irony that there is often discomfort in providing comfort. Yet, we all partake in Christ's blessings and are to serve one another.

One reason for this is that death is a common enemy. While others face it today, we all will someday unless the Lord returns before then. And we do well to be reminded that death is a defeated enemy. Medicine did not and will not defeat it; it can merely delay it. The victor over death is our Lord Jesus Christ. We share in this hope, even as we walk through the valley of death with one another.

We succumb to the medicalization of death when we leave care to doctors. Medicine deals little with families. Recall years ago that even at the birth of a baby fathers were left to pace in a waiting room while the medical professionals attended to the mother-to-be. Hospitals used to have very limited visiting hours, neglecting the emotional and social needs of patients. Medicine is learning that support for patients is beneficial to recovery, and so has become more flexible about letting others be around those who are sick.

Pastors and other spiritual family can take advantage of this to visit the sick in the hospital (very literally fulfilling Christ's commission that we mentioned at the outset of this chapter). But all of this can still leave the family neglected. Brothers and sisters in Christ need to care for the caregivers of the sick and dying, and for those who suffer loss. What would it look like if we did this a bit better?

First, the church would see this as a priority. Our chapter for pastors and leaders discussed some ways to help increase awareness of ministering to those facing death. It is difficult to respond to a problem if one does not see it as a problem. Awareness, then, is the first step for the church. Communication is key: mentioning those who are ill in church news communications. Committees might focus on tracking families facing medical challenges and serve as liaisons for the help from members of the church. This attention would ideally continue long after a death, particularly when a surviving spouse or other family members face trials in adjusting to the loss spiritually, emotionally, financially, or practically (e.g., needing transportation, having to relocate, etc.). Involving young people in this work is important, making them aware of the needs of others and strengthening their faith in light of life's realities. This will help them grow past the denial of death in our culture, and to be more aware of their own mortality and the importance of living for eternity.

Beyond this, there are a number of more specific things for the community of faith to do to care for the families of the sick, dying, and deceased. The overall goal is comfort. Recall that this word actually derives from the Latin *fortis* or strength. Thus to comfort is to be 'strong with' someone. We are to help strengthen those who walk with loved ones through death and after the death.

How do we do this? First, by being humble and honest about our finitude. We have already discussed the tension between praying for life and preparing for death, and as we comfort those close to the dying we begin by being realistic about death itself: it is inevitable and it is defeated.

We comfort these comforters by freeing them from as many everyday burdens as we can, buying back their time to be with the loved one, or to grieve well after a death. This can include the traditional provision of meals, but as needed, childcare, house cleaning and chores, transportation, yard work, and creating a space for occasional rest. Housing for out-of-town family might relieve the burden of hotel bills. There will be many unique ways to help in each individual situation that thoughtful Christians will notice. The goal is to help those who walk these valleys to have a 'carefree care'.[1]

We can invite them into our homes for a meal and just be with them. Just as the many cords of a rope make it stronger, the comfort – being strong with – of other believers encourages and strengthens those who wait or grieve. Whether in our homes or theirs, or a hospital, a key ministry is listening. As we have noted before, there are no magic words that make pain go away. Trite phrases or appeals that 'God is in control' may have truth, but might not provide comfort. Stress, anxiety, and grief are difficult enough without adding guilt by implying these sufferers are not being 'spiritual' enough. Recall once more the disastrous 'counsel' that Job received from his friends. So, just be there. Let your words be few. It may be better to ask questions than to give advice, if you are in a position where the person feels safe talking. 'Do you care to share some of your thoughts about the situation?' 'What are you

---

1. Allen Verhey, *The Christian Art of Dying: Learning from Jesus* (Grand Rapids, MI: Eerdmans), 2011; p. 381.

expecting to happen?' 'How is life different since [person] went to be with the Lord?' 'How is all of this impacting your relationship with God?' And maybe don't ask 'How can I help?' Rather, deduce something the person or family needs and offer specifically, 'Would it be okay with you if I/we did that for you? It would be an honor.'

Depending on the situation and the trust the person has in you, you may ask questions that help them walk through the tasks of dying well and coping with loss that are discussed throughout this book. Lead them gently through these things, and be patient if the person or family is hesitant to 'let go' of hope if the loved one still lives, or 'let go' of the person who has died. The critical thing is just to be present – to visit, pray, support, encourage, and, yes, comfort. Make sure they feel that they are not alone and God's people are there for them. This is particularly vital outside the crisis week of an actual death, as often support is generous then but otherwise in short supply.

A final thought in comforting the hurting and grieving in Christian community is the simple and powerful 'golden rule' our Lord gave us: 'So whatever you wish that others would do to you, do also to them, for this is the Law and the Prophets' (Matt. 7:12). Remember, you, too, will die. You, too, will endure the loss of loved ones. Ask yourself what you would want or need from others, and then do that for those who are experiencing this today. For in doing this for them, we are doing it for Christ.

❧ PRAYER ❦
Lord, grant us the courage to lean in to those in our
midst who have had a loved one die, and do unto
them as we would like them to do for us
in similar circumstances.

15

Seeking 'Closure' with a Dying Loved One

Was ever grief like mine?...

<small>George Herbert[1]</small>

My family has often been blessed to vacation on Cape Cod, Massachusetts, retreating to a milder climate to briefly escape the humid summers here in the southern United States. I recall one house we rented while there. It was gorgeously gardened with thousands of flowers in bloom, the landscaping even featuring a koi pond and several wonderful places to sit and admire the landscape and the wildlife that visited it. The inside was warm and accommodating, making for one of the most memorable stays we had on the Cape. But the time passed all too fast, and we were packing. We cleaned up our messes, took out the trash, swept the floor, hauled out our luggage and settled the finances with the owner. I traditionally take a last look around the place to make sure we have everything, but partly my motive is to mentally take a 'snapshot' of the place where we made memories together. It is my way of saying 'goodbye, and thank you.'

I still debate whether to use the word 'closure' in this chapter. It is a modern term, and often used in a psychological sense of gaining closure after the death of a loved one. One can supposedly

---

1. From *The Sacrifice* in his book, *The Temple* (1633). Last accessed 2/14/2017 at https://www.ccel.org/h/herbert/temple/Sacrifice.html

work through some stages of grief and 'close' the account of the loved one. This is an ill-conceived concept, though, as one does not forget a loved one who has died, nor is life typically the same afterward. Closure in this sense just does not happen. We will explore the grieving process more in our last section.

I am using the term 'closure' here to describe some of the things you will likely want to do before you say 'goodbye' to a cherished someone. On earth, most all things come to an end – like my vacation. Memories remain, and a longing for what is lost, but they are not forgotten and life is not the same afterward. I have fond memories of my vacation and still see the lovely house in my imagination (and a few photos we took). My memories would not be as positive had we not made peace with the homeowner when we left, however. This is a sample of the type of closure I am referring to: finishing a time of life or relationship well so that the loss is no worse than need be.

Certainly the death of one you love is a much more emotional and meaningful event than a vacation, but human relationships come to an end on earth, and these ends yield fewer conflicted memories when the closing of the relationship is done properly. As we conclude this section on walking through the last weeks and days of the life of a loved one, let us consider some things that may facilitate a simpler, cleaner ending.

Let me interject a word to those mourning the loss of the person you love even prior to his or her death – that is, those who have loved ones with Alzheimer's or other forms of dementia. This is particularly tragic as you may feel you are caring for a stranger as the person you knew has already 'died' in a sense. The disease is cruel in many ways, but one is that it may deprive you of opportunities for closure in some of the ways we will discuss. May God grant you grace in this heart-rending situation. Sometimes those with dementia are more coherent, and you might have some occasion to express some final thoughts then. If not, know that God is merciful and understands.

We have noted how each death is different, and each relationship is different, too. So, there is not a 'checklist' of things to consider that fits for everyone. Here are some suggestions for you to adapt according to your situation.

First, a person's last days are no time to let fear or apprehension get the best of you. If there is anything that you believe you need to say to the person, please say it. One of the most common regrets is failure to say things one wishes one had. You may need to confess something, or clarify something, or just make sure you told the person how much you love him or her. Evidence is strong that grief after the loss of someone you are not at peace with is more difficult.

Do you have lingering questions about something that happened between you and the loved one in the past? Now is the time to bring these up and seek clarification of any misunderstanding that might cloud the relationship.

Be vulnerable. Pride is insidious, and may keep us from doing or saying things we wish we had done. There might be a need to reconcile with a sibling, or uncle, or other family member. How precious would it be to the dying one to be informed that peace had returned to the family?

Is forgiveness for anything needed? While it is not your place to insist that the dying person forgive you, you may need to confess some things nonetheless. The goal is to know you said them, even if the person is unwilling to forgive you, or unable to grasp the situation so as to forgive you. The reverse situation may apply: you may need to forgive the loved one for something said or done. This is not the place to go into detail about the process of forgiving[2] but suffice it to say that we are to forgive those who trespass against us just as Christ forgave us (Matt. 6:12). Jesus died for our sins while we were still sinners (Rom. 5:8), not after waiting to see if we would say we are sorry.

Grief is complicated by guilt or mixed feelings toward the deceased. Searching our hearts before God is imperative to make sure that we have resolved all that we can with our loved one. Relationships are complex. I often tease my counselees by asking

---

2. A classic source on the topic is Lewis B. Smedes' *Forgive and Forget: Healing the Hurts We Don't Deserve* (New York, NY: HarperOne), 2007.

them to guess who I have argued with more than anyone. They are not really surprised when I say it is my wife. Why? Because we are the closest and spend the most time together. Any couple that communicates will have differences. There will then be many places where tension might still exist between you and someone you are close to who is dying. Take some time in prayer and make sure you have cleared the air with the person if possible, or at least in your own heart before God. Now is the time.

Another thing to consider is talking through final wishes for the loved one. Again the tendency to avoid uncomfortable conversations can keep us from doing the right thing. Depending on the situations, the family may need to clarify if there are final wishes about care, where to die, extreme measures that may or may not be used, and other medical issues. There is also need for good communication on financial arrangements and wishes, and making sure there is a valid will made. Does the person wish to make specific bequests to anyone of special items in his or her possession? Beyond the general distribution of finances, there is the meaningful gifting of special objects to loved ones, and you may want to prompt the dying one to consider if there are any requests here.

Often those who are dying might wish for certain songs to be sung at the memorial service, or for certain people to perform certain functions, or for what to do with flowers or donations. The dying person has little he or she can control, but dying knowing that you have committed to seeing through these last wishes will give peace to both of you.

In all of this you may sense an openness to death and the process of dying. This flows directly from the Christian traditions of death apart from medicalization. If we push the story of my vacation house into a metaphor, this loved one will be leaving the house of this body, and does well to prepare for the departure instead of being encouraged to pretend the stay will never end. Gently raise these questions and topics to help your beloved to get ready to go in these ways, and to talk through whatever he or she needs to say about what the 'stay' on earth has been like. Some will welcome the honesty while you may need to tread more gently with others. Still, it is best not to live in denial nor promote it for your loved one. Speak of the hope of heaven while not denying the agony of the transition to it from this life.

During the process you might consider taking a few minutes each day to keep a journal of your thoughts and prayers as you walk through this valley. This is a concrete way to make sure you are going through the process alertly and being honest with yourself and God as you do. Pray and lament as you need, and draw on family and faith community resources as you do. Pride and self-sufficiency have no place in these days. Be vulnerable.

Finally, good 'closure' includes saying goodbye. This is rarely a literal experience, unless you are at the bedside in the final minutes or in the last vestiges of a person's coherence. Really, in all we've discussed in this chapter you are saying goodbye. You may review your times together, reflecting on the ups and downs of your relationship and shared memories. You may give the dying loved one room to express hopes for you or other dear ones as they move forward. Most of all, make sure the person knows how much you love him or her, and how much the relationship has meant to you.

Consider each parting as potentially your last, saying what needs to be said. Remember how I looked around the rental house one last time before leaving? Interestingly, I still remember the last mental 'photo' of my grandmother and my father when I parted with them for the last time before they went to be with the Lord. So as you dismiss yourself from the loved one each time, be aware that this might be your goodbye and keep a mental image of it. You can replace it with a new one should you be granted another time together with the loved one.

George Herbert's poem in the epigram refers to the special grief that Jesus experienced, something that gives assurance that He understands our sorrow. None of these steps make the death of someone you love painless, but they may facilitate memories that are unclouded by guilt, regret, and pride.

❧ PRAYER ❧

Lord, we pray that You would grant each who reads
this a 'good grief' as they walk through the valley of
the shadow of death, for You are with them.

Part III

As I Am Dying

Introduction

I have seen death and talked with those near death. I have interviewed numerous adults and children who have had a loved one die, and, of course, done a considerable amount of reading on the subject. My training and background give me at least some credibility as knowing something about dying in general.

But I have not faced my own death, much less been through it. One of the challenges of addressing those who are most likely nearing death is that you have experienced more than I have. And of course, there is no one who has truly died who can instruct us. I will try to offer some helpful insights for those of you who are in the December of life, and hopefully this will encourage the rest of us as we know our day is coming, too.

There is much I believe those of you who are facing your own death can learn from other parts of this book, but the next few chapters are designed specifically for you. I write with great awe and humility, assuming that you face great challenges, doubts, pain, grief, and anxiety while at the same time holding on to the hope of life after death with our precious Savior.

16

Learning from Jesus as He Faced Death

It is the LORD. Let him do what seems good to him.

1 SAMUEL 3:18

It may seem odd at first glance that I open this with a quote from Eli as he worked with his disciple Samuel. Yet, the quote above nicely captures the overall approach we see as Jesus faced death. Beginning in the garden the night before, Jesus's struggle resolved with the words 'not my will, but yours, be done' (Luke 22:42). If we are indeed God's, then we are at His disposal – and after all, He loves us more than we love ourselves. We will see in Jesus's statements on the cross how this played out in the last hours before His death.

But to begin, consider this: what must it have been like for God Himself to face death? The paradox of this wracks my brain. Though He had had some thirty-three years to accustom Himself to life as a human being, He, too, faced death for the first time. His agony in the Garden of Gethsemane as He anticipated what was to come suggests that He is no stranger to the feelings you may have as you face the end of life.

Numerous sermon series have been preached on the seven sayings of the Savior on the cross as there is much richness in these short words. And I readily admit that they probably were not spoken primarily as guidelines on how to face death. Yet, they afford a helpful outline of some of the ways of wisdom as one

105

moves to the point of acceptance of one's final earthly fate. Let us look briefly at each.

'Father, forgive them, for they know not what they do' (Luke 23:34). There can be no greater injustice than Jesus suffered: the only sinless, perfect person who ever lived was executed as a criminal. Even worse, He is the Creator of the people who did the dirty work. If ever there was a justification for being unforgiving, this would have been it. Yet, even as He suffered at the hands of sinners, He prayed to His Father to forgive them. The implication for us is the same: any injustice – real or imagined – that we have experienced cannot compare to that which Jesus endured. If He, our Model, was forgiving, we must be also.

So as you face the end of your life, who do you need to forgive? Are there long-held grudges against family members, former co-workers, neighbors, or friends that need to be made right before you die? Pride has no place now (if it ever did). Prayerfully seek God's face and have Him show you any bitterness in your heart that needs to be addressed. If you can make actual reconciliation with others, wonderful. If you only do so in your heart before the Lord, that, too, is excellent. Even consider those who care for you. Are you angry about physicians' decisions that did not work out as you had hoped, or insensitive nursing care, or procedures that cause pain? Be forgiving to all and like Jesus, particularly those who are managing you near the end.

'Truly I say to you, today you will be with me in paradise' (Luke 23:43). This may be the most difficult of the sayings to apply to our deaths. The point I wish to make here is that Jesus, in agony and feeling forsaken, nonetheless has a word of compassion to a sinner near Him. While there are far too many ways that I am not like Jesus, one is that I would picture myself in this situation so focused on my pain and the injustice of my situation that I fear I would have little care for a fellow sufferer nearby. Not our Lord. Even at His darkest hour, He cared for others.

What would that look like for you? How are you a testimony to your family and friends in these days and hours? Even in pain and discomfort, can you find it in your heart to see their needs? What a testimony it is to our Lord when His people can reach out to others even in their time of sickness. Consider also those who care for you. It is easy to be crabby with care-givers who come to stick yet another needle into you, or who move your body in painful ways. Here is a rare opportunity to show Christ in a special way as you speak love and kindness into the lives of those around you. (And focusing on others may prove a distraction from your own discomfort!)

'He said to his mother, "Woman, behold your son!" Then he said to the disciple [John], "Behold, your mother!"' (John 19:26-27). Not only did Jesus seek forgiveness for His murderers and show compassion to a criminal, He took care of His blessed mother. Women were in a fragile place in society at that time, and Mary was already a widow. Now, her son is being killed. For all of the suffering He was enduring, Jesus saw that His mother was taken care of as He entrusted her to His beloved disciple John. It is all too easy to become wrapped up in oneself when suffering, and how much more so when facing the end of life. Yet Jesus attends to family business because of His great love for His mother.

It is also incumbent upon us to see that our families are cared for in our absence. This can start with making a will and discussing finances and housing with a spouse that will be left behind. It may involve talking with your children about how to care for your widow or widower, or how to manage the estate if you are alone at this point. The key is to die knowing that those who you cared for and who cared for you are provided for, materially, emotionally, and spiritually.

These first three statements all showed care for others, and we need to remember the source of His ability to do this: Jesus's resignation to God's will, which was death.

'My God, my God, why have you forsaken me?' (Matt. 27:46). Jesus speaks in fulfillment of Psalm 22:1, showing the depth of His anguish. The pain and suffering was one thing, but His cry shows the horror of enduring it while separated from His Father as He bore our sin. The eternal relation of love between Father and Son is suspended as Jesus suffers the consequences for our sin, bearing it Himself. Such agony cannot be imagined by us.

107

We learn here that even Jesus was honest with God about His suffering. We will discuss lament a little later, but notice here that Jesus Himself lamented His separation from the Father. You may lament leaving loved ones and valued things in this life. No need to be heroic or even stoic. God welcomes your cries of distress even as He heard those of the psalmists and His own Son.

While you may not wish to burden your family and loved ones with your sorrow, you may share it with them so they can comfort you. But there is no need to hold back with God. Express your pain, your fear, your loneliness, your despair. Because of Jesus, I believe we can say the Father is more available to you at the hour of death than He was to Jesus since you stand clothed in Christ's righteousness, whereas Jesus was distanced by bearing your sin and mine.

'I thirst' (John 19:28). These words are also spoken in fulfillment of Old Testament Scripture (Ps. 42:2 and 63:1), as did the sour wine given Him in response (Ps. 69:21). It is important to note that Jesus had declined a drink earlier that would have anesthetized Him to His suffering (Matt. 27:34). As He approaches the end, the cry seems to be simply about thirst, not anesthesia.

We see Jesus speaking up for His need, even at this late hour of life. While we are not destined to fulfill Scripture as He did, we may feel free to express our needs for physical comforts as we die. We are not bearing the sin of others, so we need not even reject anesthetics as our Savior did. With Jesus as your example, do not hesitate to ask for things you need in your last days.

'It is finished' (John 19:30). It seems that Jesus wet His throat with the sour wine so He could speak this conclusive word. We might speculate about the full significance of this brief statement, but I sense in it at least some sense of relief. The ordeal He came to earth for and shed tears over in the Garden is now at an end. He did not fight death; indeed, He may at this point have welcomed it as an end to His passion. Of course, this can also be interpreted as saying the work of salvation He came to accomplish is now finished. How wonderful and comforting a truth is this! As you face death, the punishment for your sin is finished. No hell awaits you, but only the loving arms of the Father, because Jesus finished His mission. Praise be to God.

For us, we see from this there is a time to concede that the race is run, the task finished, and the story told. Your life has reached its finish. For all the loss and sadness, there is a strain of relief and joy in knowing that your last tear is about to be shed, your last jolt of pain experienced, and your last struggle completed. I have seen this with people I have known: the day comes when they know life is finished and they are ready to 'go home' to be with the Lord. I pray you find this resolution and peace as your last breath nears.

'Father, into your hands I commit my spirit!' (Luke 23:46). Jesus once again takes the words of Scripture to His lips, this time from Psalm 31:5. As a side note, consider how many of Jesus's words were Scripture, reflecting on His knowledge of His Word, and setting an example that we would hide His Word in our hearts and find comfort in it in all our lives and also at our passing.

As the God-Man passes away and loses consciousness, there is a sense of a loss of control. He responds by making clear that He is surrendering His spirit into the loving and sovereign hands of His Father. What safer place to commend your soul at your death? We live to God and we die to Him. We wrestle to yield self-will to the will of God. Yet in the end we will lose all will and all control on our own. How blessed to follow in Jesus's steps by commending our spirit to the God who loves us more than we love ourselves.

So notice the pattern. Three of the sayings are acts of ministry in the midst of dying. One is a cry of physical need that gets a response from those around the cross. The other three are cries to His Father, one of desperation but the others show He has come to terms with His death, finished His course, and yields His spirit to God. What better model for us to have in how to manage our last days!

❧ PRAYER ❧

Father, teach me from the blessed death of Your
Son Jesus how to face death with grace and
selflessness, to the glory of Your Name.

17
Reviewing Your Life

God having in this world placed us in a sea, and troubled sea
with a continual storm, hath appointed the church for a ship,
and religion to be the stern; but there is no haven or port but
death. Death is that harbor, whither God hath designed every
one, that there he may find rest from the trouble of the world.

JEREMY TAYLOR[1]

The Puritan Richard Baxter minced no words about the hardships of life. All of us have faced numerous challenges, though
clearly some have had a harder time than others. His image of life
as a storm and the church as our ship is apropos, though some have
been in rougher waters, and some have encountered conflict in the
church. Still, there is no arguing about the final harbor of death.
It is the end of a journey, and an entrance into eternal rest and
peace. You now have the harbor in view – maybe in the distance,
and maybe moving rapidly into the foreground. As your journey
winds down, there is much wisdom in taking time to review the
journey.

The process of reflecting on one's life near its end is often called
a life review. It is a way of systematically reflecting on the journey
as a way of finding joy, peace, and comfort as life ends. In this
chapter I will encourage you to consider doing this as I offer some
suggestions on how to do this and what to cover.

---

1. *The Rule and Exercises of Holy Dying*, Section 7, last accessed 02/14/2017 at
http://www.ccel.org/ccel/taylor/holy_dying.v.vii.html.

Why do this? There are several reasons. There is a natural inclination to reflect at such a time, and this simply gives some structure to it. This can also serve as a form of worship, looking at how God has worked in your life while maybe noticing some times you have failed in your service to Him. It can be a time of thanksgiving for those who have joined you on the journey as you reflect on the roles they have played in your life. It may also be of comfort to consider how God has used you in the lives of others and His church along the way. Reflecting on your life can remind you of ways your life has made a difference. All of this hopefully will lead to a greater sense of peace with the imminence of death, and of completion at the end of the journey. If done with family or other loved ones, such reflection may also help the family be reminded of your story and maybe gain a few stories or snippets to pass along the family line. It also may help them come to greater peace with the end of your journey.

You can do a life review privately in your mind, between you and God. Often, though, using external supports may help. You might dictate some of your recollections into an audio recording, or write them if you are able. You may also bring in family members to share in the telling of the stories of your life. They may remember some anecdotes you have forgotten. They may also be helpful in walking you through the suggested topics by asking questions to get your thinking going. You may also put together a life book, which is a type of scrap book with pictures and mementos of significant life events (wedding invitations, plane tickets from enjoyable trips, etc.). You might simply ask family to provide you with photo albums from your life, or to share some they might have on electronic devices.

Whether you do your life review alone or with others, and whether or not you document, the process still will be a profound review of God's grace in your life. Along the way, you can begin to say goodbye to the people you have known and loved, either simply by reflecting on them or actually by trying to contact them. You may discover some areas in your life that are open accounts – situations where you may need to ask forgiveness or seek reconciliation. It is important to you and to others that you leave no conflicts or bitter feelings unresolved if at all possible. Don't be proud at this point. Clearing the air with others will bring you peace, be an act of obedience to God, and make grieving and moving on easier for the other persons involved. Prayerfully consider engaging in a life review, asking God for openness to celebrate His grace and to seek peace with Him and others around you as you prepare to enter the harbor at the end of your journey.

Finally, I offer a list of topics to reflect on. Take some time with each and try not only to remember events, but picture them in your mind as vividly as you can. Remember the emotions you had and the conversations you shared with others. You may even recall smells and aromas of something – your mother's home-baked bread, your wife's delicious lasagna, the salt air of the seaside, and so forth. Here are some suggestions.

Childhood and Youth

- Recall your early homes and neighborhoods. What was your room like?
- What do you remember about your parents from then? Other relatives?
- Do/did you have siblings? What were they like to live with?
- Remember any special friends. And pets.
- Any funny stories from those days?
- What activities did you participate in and enjoy (or maybe not)?
- Any vacations that were particularly memorable?
- Were you involved in any sports, clubs, or other groups in high school?
- Recall early dates and boy or girl friends.
- What was school like for you? Any success or failure stories?
- What was your church involvement?

- Do you recall becoming a Christian? (This may come later in your story)
- Were there valued mentors or church leaders who helped you as you matured?
- What was your spiritual life like then?

Adulthood

- Did you go to college? What were your experiences there like?
- Who were your college friends?
- How did your walk with Christ change as you moved out on your own?
- How did you meet your spouse? Recall stories of your courtship and marriage.
- Any memorable experiences like trips, concerts, etc.?
- How did marriage change your life?
- How did you choose your career? Reflect on the jobs you have held. Which did you like the best? What were your relationships like with bosses and co-workers?
- What accomplishments did you make on the job?
- Would you have followed a different job path if you had your time again?
- Remember the births of your children. How did each in turn enrich your life?
- What are some of your favorite stories from the days your children were little and in the home?
- How did your marriage change over the years? What struggles did you have? (And in some cases, what led to the divorce?)
- Who have been your most faithful friends? Why?
- What ministries have you been a part of? Recall special moments in those.

- Who were the most powerful spiritual influences in your life? Even consider those who may have been influential through books.

- What are some of your fondest memories from each decade of your life?

- Picture the homes and towns you have lived in.

Later Life

- Think through your journey with Christ and how you have grown and/or struggled in your walk with Him along the way.

- What was retiring from work like for you?

- What did you miss about your job?

- How did changes in your health affect you?

- What have you done to cope with these?

- What loved ones have you lost as you aged? How did you manage those losses?

- What changes have come in your family?

- What have you enjoyed about your grandchildren and great-grandchildren? What is a favorite story about each?

- What activities have been meaningful to you?

- How has your spiritual life changed as you have aged?

- How has your marriage matured? Or, what has widow(er)-hood been like for you?

- How has your involvement in church and ministry changed in your later years?

- Reflect on what you wish you had done differently?

- Who have been the most important people in your life? Why?

- Who are some people you have had conflict with? Was it resolved? Is there anything you can do now to make peace?

- What were some of your happiest times?

- How have you sensed God's faithfulness to you in your aging and illness? Or how have you struggled with this?

- Think of five Bible verses that are particularly precious to you.

- Think of five songs that have been special to you.

- Is there any business you need to take care of – financially, spiritually, relationally – before the day of your death?

❧ PRAYER ❦

Dear Jesus, we thank You that You know how death feels, and never leave us nor forsake us. Thank You for guiding us on the voyage of our lives. You have been faithful through good times and bad, and we know You will not desert us as we near the final harbor.

18

Lament and Hope

*No affliction is greater than despair ... against
this hope is to be opposed.*

Jeremy Taylor[1]

How am I supposed to feel? This is a common question I hear and it honestly troubles me a bit. For all of my years of experience as a psychologist, I cannot say that there is a directory for what one should feel in a given situation. And even if there were, few if any of us have the skill (or whatever it takes) to make us feel the way we are supposed to. How we feel in certain situations may say something about us, but we really can't dictate how we will feel. In facing the end of one's mortal life it is easy for Christians to slip into platitudes on how one 'ought' to feel, leaving any who feel differently to wonder if they are guilty of some lack of faith or depth in their relationship with God and that this is the reason for their not feeling the 'right' way.

I do not want to be one who speaks to another who is dying and tells you how to feel at this point. I have no right as I, like everyone else who is not near death, have not faced it myself. What I offer, however, are some thoughts on the extremes of emotion that you may experience, and offer some biblical support for them.

I recall the very intentional shift in emotions during the funeral service of an African-American friend's mother. The service began very somberly with sadness and grief given full place. But as the

---

1. *The Rule and Exercises of Holy Dying*, Section III, last accessed 02/14/2017 at www.ccel.org/ccel/taylor/holy_dying.v.iii.html.

service progressed, mourning was turned to hope as the loss of this woman was turned into gratefulness for her happiness in heaven. Using that as a model, I will talk about lament then offer a few words of hope, but by no means is this meant to be a 'prescription' for how your emotions will go. It hopefully serves only as some permission to lament and as a reminder that there is hope.

Lament is a rare word in churches these days. The culture seems to demand that sermons be happy and practical, coaching us on how to thrive in our world and feel good in the process. The result is that many Christians are unaware of how much lament is in the Bible. A great resource for this is Michael Card's book, *A Sacred Sorrow: Reaching Out to God in the Lost Language of Lament*[2] and I will draw some of the ideas that follow from his outline.

The Bible is full of lament. The most familiar resource for lament is the Psalms. David, the author of many of these, was no stranger to heartache. He was pursued by Saul, had many 'family issues' and faced numerous hardships – all after he was told he would be king. He shares lament in many of the Psalms (and Card has these in an appendix for the reader's convenience). These were occasioned by his own sin, by being deceived, by seeing God's kingdom struggle and by various persecutions. Maybe most poignant for our current topic is Psalm 22. Jesus quoted this on the cross, so its applicability to death seems warranted. Here is a section of it (v. 1-11):

> *My God, my God, why have you forsaken me?*
> *Why are you so far from saving me, from the words of my*
>   *groaning?*
> *O my God, I cry by day, but you do not answer,*
> *and by night, but I find no rest.*
> *Yet you are holy,*
> *enthroned on the praises of Israel.*
> *In you our fathers trusted;*
> *they trusted, and you delivered them.*
> *To you they cried and were rescued;*
> *in you they trusted and were not put to shame.*

---

2. Colorado Springs (CO, USA, NavPress), 2005.

But I am a worm and not a man,
scorned by mankind and despised by the people.
All who see me mock me;
they make mouths at me; they wag their heads;
'He trusts in the Lord*; let him deliver him;*
let him rescue him, for he delights in him!'
Yet you are he who took me from the womb;
you made me trust you at my mother's breasts.
On you was I cast from my birth,
and from my mother's womb you have been my God.
Be not far from me,
for trouble is near,
and there is none to help.

One more famed than David for troubles is Job. It is hard to even imagine the woes of his life as his family, possessions, and health were virtually wiped out in almost an instant. While he came to peace with God eventually, it was not without lament over the turn his life had taken. Maybe nowhere in the book is this more evident than in chapter 7:

Has not man a hard service on earth,
and are not his days like the days of a hired hand?
Like a slave who longs for the shadow,
and like a hired hand who looks for his wages,
so I am allotted months of emptiness,
and nights of misery are apportioned to me.
When I lie down I say, 'When shall I arise?'
But the night is long,
and I am full of tossing till the dawn.
My flesh is clothed with worms and dirt;
my skin hardens, then breaks out afresh.
My days are swifter than a weaver's shuttle
and come to their end without hope.
'Remember that my life is a breath;
my eye will never again see good.
The eye of him who sees me will behold me no more;

119

while your eyes are on me, I shall be gone.
As the cloud fades and vanishes,
so he who goes down to Sheol does not come up;
he returns no more to his house,
nor does his place know him anymore.
'Therefore I will not restrain my mouth;
I will speak in the anguish of my spirit;
I will complain in the bitterness of my soul. (vv. 1-11)

Though Job was not dying, his 'symptoms' sound as though he was – and likely at this point he may have wished he were dead. Desperate and in misery, he pours out the complaint of his soul to God. While at points he misunderstands God, his Lord eventually responds to his plea. Many of these words may capture your experience, and so may inspire a prayer of lament from you. God is sovereign and can take it.

Jeremiah is another servant of God who had a tough go of it. What a life calling: to prophesy of the doom of the nation he loves, even as God makes it clear the people won't listen. Arrested and put into a pit along the way, Jeremiah stays faithful. However, his mission gets to him and leads to some remarkably passionate words in chapter 20. After even accusing God of deceiving him in verse 7, his lament crescendos to this climax (vv. 14-18):

Cursed be the day
on which I was born!
The day when my mother bore me,
let it not be blessed!
Cursed be the man who brought the news to my father,
'A son is born to you,'
making him very glad.
Let that man be like the cities
that the LORD overthrew without pity;
let him hear a cry in the morning
and an alarm at noon,
because he did not kill me in the womb;
so my mother would have been my grave,

and her womb forever great.
Why did I come out from the womb
to see toil and sorrow,
and spend my days in shame?

You may identify with some of the potent thoughts of this passage. God did not desert Jeremiah as a result of these words. He knows the struggles we face, and is with us even as we walk through them.

And then there is Jesus Himself, a man of sorrows and acquainted with grief (Isa. 53:3). Here we find God Himself among us and treated wrongly. His life was suffering, for just to live in a sinful world must have been painful for God in human flesh. I remember a comment by theologian Marva Dawn who noted the early Apostles' Creed lacked punctuation, and so noted that the line 'suffered under Pontius Pilate' might also read 'suffered, under Pontius Pilate was crucified'. This brings out that Jesus's suffering was more than just on the cross, but throughout His earthly life.

Jesus is a realist, not a spiritual leader who promises health and wealth. In fact, He promises us that we will lament. John 16:20 quotes Jesus, 'Truly, truly, I say to you, you will weep and lament, but the world will rejoice. You will be sorrowful, but your sorrow will turn into joy.' Notice here that Jesus actually promises we will experience weeping and lament. He is not surprised by that. While there are many reasons for such lament, the approach of the end of life may be included in this.

So, grief and lament are not alien to the Bible. It is not a book that promises giddy happiness and constant smiles. It is a gritty, honest book showing us that God knows our pain, struggles, doubts, and anxieties.

Jesus's words above point us to a final point for this chapter: this sorrow will turn to joy. The Bible stares this sorrow square in the eyes and is brutally honest about the suffering of some very godly people. Yet, there is the hope of joy ahead. 1 Thessalonians 4:13 reminds us that we are not to grieve as those who have no hope. Even Jesus eyed hope as a way to walk through His death, for Hebrews 12:2 hints at His strategy: it was for the joy set before Him that He endured the cross.

Lament as you need to. Be honest and don't hide your feelings from God, no matter what they are. Express them to those close to you to the extent you believe they can accept and handle them. But in so doing, do so with hope that suffering will end and you will be with Jesus. The loss we suffer is easily worth the glory of being with God. It may take some work to see this hope, and other parts of this book may help you along the way. I close with the words of a song that has meant much to me through the years. I pray that I can say these honestly in my last days, and that you can, too.

Home Where I Belong

(Pat Terry and B. J. Thomas) 1976 Copyright Pat Terry

They say that heaven's pretty
And living here is too
But if they said that I
would have to choose between the two
I'd go home, going home, where I belong

And sometimes when I'm dreaming
It comes as no surprise
That if you look and see
The homesick feeling in my eyes
I'm going home, going home, where I belong

While I'm here I'll serve him gladly
And sing him all my songs
I'm here, but not for long
And when I'm feeling lonely
And when I'm feeling blue
It's such a joy to know that
I am only passing through
I'm headed home, going home, where I belong

And one day I'll be sleeping,
When death knocks on my door
And I'll awake and find that
I'm not homesick anymore
I'll be home, going home, where I belong.

19
Temptations and Virtues in the Face of Dying

*Too many contemporary believers
... tend to reduce the religious life to
its attractive dimension, eliminating
the experience of God as* mysterium
tremendum *[terrible mystery]. I think
the dying frequently know better.*

ALLEN VERHEY[1]

We have noted how our culture hides death from everyday people, and the church even joins in this conspiracy at times. Yet, for one who is dying, there is no hiding except in denial. If you are reading this, it is unlikely you are denying that death is coming before very long. As one faces death more honestly and directly, the cliché phrases of the Christian faith may not satisfy as they once did. 'Ah, but won't heaven be wonderful.' 'They're in a better place.' 'Death is defeated.' All of these are true, but they are easily used to skim the surface of actually facing death and the challenges that lie in the process.

Verhey's valuable book traces themes from a fifteenth century Christian text called *Ars Moriendi*, or the art of dying. It portrayed in pictures the challenges facing the dying believer and the comfort

---

1. Allen Verhey, *The Christian Art of Dying: Learning from Jesus* (Grand Rapids, MI: Eerdmans), 2011; p. 142.

of Christ in the midst of these. This was prior to the medicalization of death, and assumed people took on the role of one dying, not just one who is sick and will only die if medicine fails. It looked higher to God as the One who is in control of the process, and viewed death as simultaneously a comfortable and terrifying process. The dying person may know faith in a more profound way than others. By facing the temptations of dying and demonstrating the virtues of so doing, faith is increased and demonstrated to others.

The goal for a Christian in the trying days of mortal illness is to bear witness (literally be a martyr, a witness), 'by his patient endurance of suffering to his confidence in God and in the grace of God and to his love of God above all else' (Verhey, p. 124). To do this, one must, in God's grace, overcome temptations and demonstrate virtues. The *Ars Moriendi* identifies these, and we will follow Verhey's description of these and add some comments.

Losing versus Keeping Faith

Without faith it is impossible to please God (Heb. 11:6), so this is the root of the Christian life at which the devil will strike. He must be resisted (1 Pet. 5:9), especially in one's last days when the adversities of illness test belief. Today's shallow spiritual understanding of God may make Christians vulnerable to difficult times as we miss the strong biblical thread about suffering (e.g. Phil. 3:10-11) and mistakenly assume that hard times reflect the absence of God. Rather, they are times to learn the terrible mystery of God – how saints have walked with Him through terrible times and learned of His grace in the midst of suffering. There are multiple biblical examples of this: from Job, to David, to Stephen, to Paul. Church history has countless stories of Christians who stayed faithful despite daunting circumstances and opposition.

The response to doubts is to make a point of identifying these for what they are, and then to resist the assault of the enemy. Reciting familiar Scriptures or the Apostles' Creed can affirm your faith. Reflect on the times of God's faithfulness in your life, or other adversities you endured where He proved faithful. Pray for grace to trust Him in this last battle.

Hebrews is addressed to suffering Christians and is famed for the faith chapter (11) that details the heroics of people of faith, many of whom did not see the promises fulfilled until after death. Notice how blunt it is about the tragic ends many of these saints met (vv. 35-40). Their fates were not inconsistent with having pleased God through faith. Your end should be no different. The author speaks to these suffering believers just after noting their faithfulness in the past: 'Therefore do not throw away your confidence, which has a great reward. For you have need of endurance, so that when you have done the will of God you may receive what is promised' (10:35-36). Pray, then, for faith to endure and be confident in the midst of adversity. Faith is a God-given virtue, and He will never leave nor forsake you (Deut. 31:6).

Despair versus Hope

As you come more directly face-to-face with your death, the devil may call to remembrance your sins and failures and even make you despair of the hope of heaven. This can add spiritual agony to the physical agony you may be experiencing. You may have long believed these sins and failures were forgiven, but now that the end is near you may have thoughts that you are not forgiven. Or you may despair of the shortcomings of your life and how you wish you had acted differently along the way. These thoughts can lead to confession instead of despair. You may even use them to prompt efforts to reconcile with someone before you part this life.

The virtue that will withstand despair is hope, for the goal of these thoughts is to cause you to die in despair rather than in hope, missing an opportunity to glorify God by the witness your death bears to Him. Comfort and hope is found in the profound forgiveness shown to so many in the Bible. I love how God did not give us hyper-spiritualized heroes. He showed us their failures. Abraham lied about Sarah and even offered her up as his sister, expecting her to be defiled as a result. Moses struck the rock and became frustrated with the people of God. David's sins of murder and adultery are only the tip of the iceberg of his failures.

125

Jesus calls a corrupt tax collector (Matthew), is followed by Mary Magdalene who apparently had a past, and forgives a criminal even as he is paying the death penalty. Peter deserts and doubts Jesus, and Paul is called after overseeing the murders of some of the earliest Christians.

I doubt your life can have much worse than this in it. Your hope is not in your good works any more than theirs was. Rather, all of us hope in the forgiveness wrought by Jesus on the cross, *and* the prospect of being joined with Him as a result of His resurrection from the dead. Focus on these biblical truths to resist ruminating about your failures.

One last word on hope. Take hope in how Jesus's death and the deaths of the martyrs bear witness to the fact that, as Verhey says, 'some things were more valuable than ease, some duties more compelling than survival' (p. 150). Medicalization of death may cause us to despair because we are 'losing' the battle for life. A more Christian take on this, evident in the *Ars Moriendi*, is that our deaths are welcomed as a way of demonstrating right to the end of life the grace of God and our surrender to Him.

Impatience versus Patience/Love

It is easy to be tempted to be impatient in the midst of suffering, being anxious either for a cure or to end the pain quickly by death. While modern medicine is helpful in relieving some pain, in many cases there can still be anguish and misery in serious illness. Pain is formidable, but fatigue, loss of bodily functions, loss of the pleasures of eating or simple entertainments, and even increased difficulty in thinking can all lead to impatience. If impatience has its way, it can lead to lessening our love for God because He doesn't resolve the suffering as quickly as we wish.

In contrast, patience (or long-suffering in older translations) is a fruit of the Spirit (Gal. 5:22), and a characteristic of love (1 Cor. 13:4). How can one be patient in the midst of chronic suffering? Faith gives meaning to suffering. Consider the pangs of childbirth. Here a mother chooses to endure great suffering because of the new life that will come as a result. This is similar to death where the suffering of the believer at the end of life ends with entrance into life in the presence of Christ. The happiness and joy that await are immeasurable compared to the suffering in this life. Know that it is the love of God that walks with you through this transition. As you are patient in the love of God, you are again a witness to God to those around you. This is a special opportunity to demonstrate to others the grace and love of God. What a legacy to leave here as you move into new life that awaits!

Pride versus Humility

We have seen that thinking may lead to doubt and despair in these dark days. But for some the opposite may occur: a sense of excessive pride in the life you have lived or the relationships you've made or the money you have made. This may be fueled if others come around and praise you for what you've meant to them or done in your life.

The response to this is humility, knowing that any genuine good you have done has been Christ working in you by His grace. You need not minimize things you have accomplished – just make sure you and others know you attribute them to your great God.

Avarice versus 'Letting Go'

One thing that may become manifest as you face death is how much you love the things of the world and long to hold on to them. We have all heard 'you can't take it with you' but now that is a reality more than just a saying. If you feel yourself clinging to things, the virtue is to let go of them. Your physical existence is coming to an end for now; only the spiritual will go with you.

But there is also a need for letting go of relationships, too. Verhey explains:

> Words of gratitude and praise, requests for forgiveness and the grant-ing of forgiveness, provision for their future well-being, and words of love and affection – all of that and more belong to letting go. (p. 154-5)

Don't be caught up trying to hold onto relationships as if there will not be an end soon (at least for a while). Verhey's list is a good 'checklist' for you to review prayerfully. Do not fail to leave a meaningful and complete 'goodbye' to loved ones because you struggle to let go. They, too, are in God's hands, and He will take care of them once you are gone.

I pray these virtues will be given to you by the grace of God as you finish your journey, and that your final days are a witness to that grace before family, friends, your church community, and the medical staff around you. This is one of the most opportune times you have had to glorify God. Use it well.

A Final Word to the Dying

We bring to a close the devotions intended for the individual who is dying, and that may well be you. If you are able and care to, you may read on in the book and find some encouragement there. But in the spirit of good endings, let me join those who love you and know you in thanking you for doing your part for the kingdom of God. We likely have never met, but we will one day. We are family, united in Christ. I will follow you soon, or maybe this book is still used after my death and I have gone to be with God ahead of you. Regardless, I thank God for calling you to Himself and to your rest. I pray you finish well, and can say with the apostle Paul: 'I have fought the good fight, I have finished the race, I have kept the faith. Henceforth there is laid up for me the crown of righteousness, which the Lord, the righteous judge, will award to me on that day, and not only to me but also to all who have loved his appearing' (2 Tim. 4:7-8).

You are entering sacred space, and you are not alone. This time is special not only for you, but for God, for 'Precious in the sight of the LORD is the death of his saints' (Ps. 116:15). Even in the suffering that may lie ahead, never forget how precious this transition is to God – and He will not forsake you. Grace and peace be with you now and forever more. Amen.

Part IV

Mourning a Death Out of Season

Introduction

Our meditations change focus now, moving from preparing for a death to grieving a death. Much of our discussion has focused on being with and serving one who is dying and in getting ready for the death to come, both for the dying person and his or her loved ones. Now come the grief and mourning that follow the loss.

We first look at the special grief that comes with an unexpected loss where much of the last two sections does not apply. There is little or no warning as someone we love is taken, most often before they have reached old age.

We will consider the uniquenesses of grief in these cases as we consider some of the major types of death out of season. A particularly sensitive area is children and death. We will step into the grief and coping of a brother in Christ who lost a child, then consider the ways children grieve.

20

Grieving Sudden and Unexpected Deaths

The death of a beloved is an amputation.

MADALEINE L'ENGLE[1]

Lewis captures so much in this statement from his work where he shared of the loss of his wife of a mere four years. She died of cancer at the age of forty-five. In our day, we expect to live much longer than forty-five years and that marriage will be far more than four years in duration. His was a loss out of season, a death at a place in life where one does not normally expect it to come. While all losses are hard, there is more of an expectation of death after one is old and has lived a full life. Dying in old age is more easily accepted, and seen as more normal. Losses that come earlier in life, or suddenly, or both, are harder to cope with as a rule as they are seen as particularly poignant.

For our purposes, a death out of season is one where there is a greater sense of unfairness or inappropriateness. It can be an early death, a tragic death, or one that is both. It is a death that may evoke anger and frustration because of the timing, and may preclude closure and bracing oneself for it by its suddenness.

There are several categories of such deaths out of season. Many parents and their families grieve lives that never see the light of

---

1. In her Foreword to *C. S. Lewis, A Grief Observed* (New York: HarperCollins), 1994; XII.

day – literally – when infants in the womb are miscarried. For Christians who see each life as ordained by God, and life beginning at conception, miscarriage is painful. Hopes and plans are hardly formulated in the minds of parents before being dashed by a word from a doctor.

The death of children is also especially painful. We hear a story of one parent who endured this in the next chapter, but all who go through this have a special grief. Children can die from disease, particularly cancer, or from accidents. They never reach maturity and we lament the sense that they never had a chance. This was a much more familiar refrain earlier in history and as many as half of children born did not make it to adulthood at points in the past due to illness and poor medical care. Because of our greater knowledge and technology we almost take it for granted that children will live to be adults, so when a child's life is cut short it has its unique agony. I would be remiss not to note, too, the pain of older parents who outlive a child who dies in adulthood. It seems unnatural for a parent to outlive a child, and to do so is to experience a rare grief.

Many lives are taken prematurely in accidents of various kinds. Automobile accidents likely are the most common cause, but work-related accidents, freak occurrences, stumbles and mistakes while working at home or outdoors are other types of death that are premature and give little or no warning to the victim or to the family. Similar to this are those who have unexpected and sudden medical problems. It is not unusual to hear of someone in the prime of life dying of a sudden aneurism, heart attack, or stroke. Finally, many die from weather or other nature-related events that overpower us.

Others are killed by malicious intent. Acts of terrorism are all too common and spreading to even smaller venues. My small town in Tennessee still grieves five fallen armed service members who were killed in 2015. Less common in the West, but likely to become more common, is premature death by martyrdom. I heard a news item recently saying that it is estimated that 90,000 Christians were killed because of their faith in 2016. Other random killings take lives, as individuals strike out against society by slaying people in movie theaters, schools, and even churches. Some good people die while being robbed, or are slain by someone driving while intoxicated. There are too many ways this might happen to list.

Possibly the hardest of all deaths to grieve is one that is self-inflicted. Who can measure the horror of those who learn of a child or spouse or parent or fellow church member who has taken his or her own life? Grief here may well be mixed with anger, regret, and even guilt. Christians likely do not give the attention to this horrendous problem that it deserves.

So there are many types of deaths that occur out of season, and they bring with them special circumstances of grieving that we will discuss briefly.

Such deaths often carry with them a degree of shock and sudden-ness. Much of Part II of this book was dedicated to helping people walk with a loved one during his or her last days, but those who lose a loved one suddenly will have little or no time to brace themselves and prepare for the event. The sense of shock may conflict with grief and even delay it.

This leads directly to the potential problem of more complicated grief that may last longer. You will not find in this book a set of stages or steps for grief as I believe each individual follows a unique course. The famous set of stages of Elizabeth Kübler-Ross begins with denial, and in deaths out of season, the denial may be stronger than usual. We can easily accept that an older person is ill and dying, but those faced by such atypical deaths struggle simply to admit what has happened. Grieving may have to await a process of coming to terms with what has happened.

A death from illness affords time for the person and those around him or her to adjust to the impending death. This allows time to review the life together or alone, and to make arrangements for funeral, burial, and disposition of the estate. Sudden deaths give no time for this, and saddle the loved ones with having to make such arrangements while still in shock. Certainly the church should prayerfully find ways to rally to support those in this overwhelming situation.

Most poignantly, a death out of season may leave those who remain without a sense of having bade farewell to the deceased loved one. Something of a good-bye may take place at a viewing of the body or a funeral, but not one that can be affirmed by the lost loved one. Writing a letter to enclose in the casket or something of that sort may aid the individual in expressing thoughts and feelings that did not get to be shared.

For many deaths out of season, the survivors may find themselves reliving last days and trying to produce explanations. 'If only he had left for work ten minutes later' or 'If only the light had been red instead of green' or 'If only I had been there, I could have done something.' All the 'what ifs' and 'if onlys' in the world will not bring back a loved one. These are natural human efforts to try to regain a sense of control when something happened over which one had absolutely no control. Many times the survivor will try to think of a way to assume responsibility, or to blame someone or something else. Blame may be aimed at God as well, and there the language of biblical lament may be useful, for God is indeed sovereign over life and death (Deut. 32:39). The control in the situation will be found in the all-powerful God who is not surprised by death.

Even if we concede that God is in control, that still leaves us with another common question when encountering deaths out of season: Why? The search for control then becomes a search for meaning. If it had to happen, what did it accomplish? Did it help someone? There is obvious honor in a soldier dying by jumping on a hand grenade to save a comrade, but what is served when a Christian college student is killed by a drunk driver? While we will perhaps lack the understanding to grasp God's purpose in it, we can hope that after a period of lament we will eventually come to trust His wisdom in doing what he did. We believe He works everything together for good (Rom. 8:28), but we take that on faith in many cases as God does not explain it to us. We may say with the old hymn, 'We will understand it better bye and bye.'

Another special aspect of grief for those who lose someone out of season is a subsequent sense of insecurity. A spouse who might have been in the same wreck but survived may have post-traumatic symptoms and survivor guilt. A child may fear every storm if a parent was killed in a tornado. Sudden losses can leave survivors with a sense of insecurity – a heightened sense that the world is not a safe place. If taken to the extreme, this can lead to psychological problems. Loved ones and church leaders aware of this can notice it and guide them to help.

Finally, there may be greater financial and lifestyle problems that follow. If a deceased husband was the primary source of income, the widow may have her housing situation threatened and be anxious about how she will survive financially. Recall that the first deacons were appointed to serve widows (Acts 6), and a ministry-minded church will be quick to step in to help any who may be affected in similar ways.

Those bereaved suddenly may go through more emotions in the grieving process, including anger, guilt, depression, and despair. They may also be at greater risk for a crisis in faith as they wrestle with God's role in the tragedy. If you are one of those in this situation, please do not be shy to express your frustrations to God. Read the chapter on lament earlier in the book and take some of the words from those, or other laments, to help you express your frustration with God. He is mindful that we are but dust, and can take our doubts. For those who are walking with these folks, *please* avoid pious platitudes like 'God must have had a reason' and such. Be with the people and be faithful to them as they walk this dark valley.

Death is always tragic, but the complications of death out of season challenge both the survivors and those who minister to them. May God grant special grace to all of you during this period of darkness.

21

A Child's Death
Out of Season

Rev. Robert Row[1]

When the illness of his daughter became graver Martin Luther said, 'I love her very much. But if it is thy will to take her, dear God, I shall be glad to know that she is with thee.'

MARTIN LUTHER, as his daughter Magdalene was dying[2]

At 2:44 a.m. on February 17, 2000, Emily took her first breath of air and everything looked great. She was a healthy newborn who we had immediately fallen in love with even though we had only known her for seconds. Little did we know that the Lord would use this little girl as an instrument of grace in our lives in ways we could have never imagined.

It was only hours before we learned that one of the doctors had heard a heart murmur so the pediatric cardiologist had been called in. The cardiologist discovered that Emily had a hole in her heart and that she also had Transposition of the Great Arteries. We were devastated, scared, and in shock. Our family and pastor were there with us and we could only cry out to God and the questions began

---

1. Rev. Row is the Pastor of Children and Families at First Presbyterian Church in Chattanooga, Tennessee. He is married and the father of five children, including Emily. He graciously agreed to write this chapter to share his story of Emily's brief life.

2. Table Talk #5494; September 1542.

to flood our hearts. Emily was transported to a specialty hospital and early the next morning we were given the full news about her heart. God had given Emily one of the most complex hearts they had ever seen! Several heart surgeries were to follow, beginning at 10 days old. We spent countless hours crying and praying for God to heal her. God enabled us to focus on Emily despite the tumult around her. There were several moments where we thought that her life in this world was coming to an end. For one 36 to 48 hour period Emily had an intensive care doctor at her bedside with three intensive care nurses constantly working on her. They monitored her vital signs and were constantly giving her blood products to compensate for the tremendous blood loss because of a surgical procedure that didn't work. Our whole family spent the night in the hospital because we were told that Emily might not make it through the night. We read Scripture to her and prayed for her. Our prayers were more intense than any other time in our life. We begged and pleaded, 'Stop the bleeding Lord, please!' Emily was bleeding so much that the three nurses could hardly keep up. She was losing blood as fast as they could replace it. This is only one scene from a grueling effort to save her.

We trusted that God was ultimately in control and that Emily's days were numbered by him (Ps. 139:16). The hard part was that we weren't expecting those days to be so few. She lived one hundred and seven days to be exact. God's sovereign hand was on Emily, directing the hands of the surgeons and directing every beat of Emily's heart. God was not surprised at what happened; He wasn't thrown a curve ball. He was there, directly involved in our lives and Emily's. He was not, as Bette Midler's song says, 'Watching from a distance'. He was holding us all and especially Emily close to His heart and in the palm of His hand; leading, guiding, comforting, and orchestrating all that was happening. He was certainly able to understand our grief, for He too knew what it was like to lose an only child.

Through many medical procedures, Emily developed a fungal infection in her blood stream and we waited to see if her heart was strong enough to come off life support. Two doctors told us that Emily was starting to show signs of weakening and turning blue, which meant her little heart wasn't pumping hard enough to get oxygen to the rest of her body. Only through the peace and presence of God were we able to hold ourselves up. We went in to see her knowing it was the last time we would spend with her this side of eternity. I looked up at my wife and said: 'Do you realize what's happening?' and she said, 'yes' as tears poured from our hearts. My wife stood back just holding her face in shock. I held her tight and told her to talk to Emily and tell her everything she wanted her to know. As we both talked to her we told her that we loved her and that she would be with Jesus soon and everything would be okay. Towards the end all I could do was sing a lullaby by Michael Card based on the Aaronic Benediction in Numbers 6:24-26, 'The LORD bless you and keep you; the LORD make his face to Shine upon you and be gracious to you; the LORD lift up his countenance upon you and give you peace.' We will always wonder what the Lord was doing with her those last moments. We experienced the heart of God as He was right there in our midst, feeling our hurt and pain and upholding us in the midst of it all as we experienced the pain of death in a fallen world. We imagined Him reaching out His hand and picking Emily up and telling her it's time to come home. It was time for our sweet little baby girl to go home to be with the Lord for eternity. That very hour Emily was in the arms of her Savior as she passed from this life into the next.

We knew difficult times were to follow, especially arriving at home without our little girl and seeing her room all ready for her. The grieving process had begun. Many things have gone through our minds since Emily's death and God has taught us a tremendous amount, although we wish that these lessons could be taught in another way. The probing question will always be: why? We know that the answer to that will come slowly and will not be fully understood until we meet the Lord in the air. Healthy grieving is coming to the realization that Jesus sympathizes with our weaknesses and understands our frame. He knows what loss is and understands the frailty that asks questions and longs for answers that can't be fully grasped this side of heaven. The questions that we have about the death of someone we love are natural. Many have suggested to us over the years that they don't think a Christian should ask the 'why' questions of God's providence. Personally I have asked a lot of why questions, and not because I don't believe that He works all things to the good of those who love Him and have been called according to His purpose (Rom. 8:28). No, the reason I ask those questions is that I believe God is the only one who has the answers to those questions and He is big enough to handle my questions, my doubts, my fears, my objections. The Psalms are full of this reality. (Pss. 6:3; 10:1; 13:1-2; 31:9; 42:5, 11; 88:14; 143:11).

This grappling with God over big questions magnifies our need for a Savior and the provisions of His Word. I know that I am prone to wander, O Lord, I feel it. And death is the time in which emotions are so raw that we 'feel' our sense of great loss and the questions that flow from that are normal – the Lord uses even our doubts and big questions to sanctify us. We have a limited knowledge of God's plan and no guarantee of tomorrow, but we can only cast our fears on Him and trust that all our days are ordained for us before one of them comes to be (Ps. 139:16). Some people have asked us 'are you not angry with God?' and our response has always been 'How can we do anything else but run to him? Running away is not a comforting option at all.' God understands our questions like 'Lord you knit her together in her mother's womb (Ps. 139:13), but why did you leave a couple stitches out and get a couple crossed in her heart?' God even understands our struggle with anger, but as I was reminded by a friend, 'God is bigger than my anger and questions.' He will not change, He will not waiver, He will not even flinch when I turn and run from Him. For His love for me is infinite and unchanging and does not depend on our love for Him.

Grieving the loss of a child is a process of mourning what we think might have been; a grief that longs to see her walk, talk, play, graduate from high school, get married, and so forth. It is a grieving over a future that will never be, one that God had not ordained. This kind of grief is different from the grief of the loss of a parent or grandparent that has lived a 'full life'. That kind of grief is one that looks back more than forward. Typical grief remembers a life lived whereas the process of mourning the death of child is a grief that strains to remember the brevity of the lifespan, and wonders what could have been, a fleshly sense of a life cut short.

As we search for the answers the Scriptures are quick to remind us, in the midst of that struggle, that through the resurrection of Jesus we find our hope. Our hope is grounded in the reality that death could not hold Him, and because it could not hold Him it will not hold those who are united to Him. Faith unites us to Christ in death and also unites us to Him in His resurrection life. The resurrection is the seal of our justification and the bedrock of our hope in life and in death both now and forever. It's because of the resurrection of Jesus that death no longer carries a sting. Because of the resurrection, when death comes hope lies close at hand.

When we experience a loved one's death the veil between this life and the next is almost transparent. Death brings eternal perspective to our often finite and temporal thinking. His grace in death leads us to think more often on things that are above, to think on the Lord Jesus Christ and His Kingdom. I distinctly remember the veil between this life and the next being almost translucent when Emily died, like I was able to literally peer into Heaven. Eternity seemed so close at hand.

Death reminds us that we are instruments in the hands of our Redeemer for His purposes and for His Kingdom. The grieving process reminds us that each life is significantly woven into His grand story of redemption. Death forces us to grapple for clarity of God's purposes for us individually and corporately in His Kingdom. The Apostle Paul understood this perspective. After considering all of his life accomplishments as rubbish, he said 'that I may know him and the power of his resurrection, and may share his sufferings, becoming like him in his death, that by any means possible I may attain the resurrection from the dead.' Paul goes on to say that he hasn't yet obtained it but that he presses on to 'make it my own … forgetting what lies behind and straining forward to what lies ahead,' he pressed on 'toward the goal for the prize of the upward call of God in Christ Jesus. Let those of us who are mature think this way …' (Phil. 3:10-15).

What is the goal, the prize of the upward call? What is this thing that Paul presses on to make his own? The answer is found in what Christ Jesus has made His own, 'the resurrection from the dead.' Paul's eternal perspective on this life transforms the way he lives. Every ounce of his being strives for that one thing: to share with his Savior in the resurrection from the dead. Paul later says, '… join in imitating me and keep your eyes on those who walk according to the example you have in us' (Phil. :3:17). 'If the Spirit of him who raised Jesus from the dead dwells in you, he who raised Christ Jesus from the dead will also give life to your mortal bodies through his Spirit who dwells in you' (Rom. 8:11). Our hope is found in this beautiful union we have with our Savior that His life is ours, His death is ours, and His resurrection is ours (Rom. 6:1-11). Therefore, grieving the loss of someone we love changes us, and by God's grace our gaze goes from the temporal to the eternal. Because of our union with Christ and His resurrection we grieve not as ones who have no hope (1 Thess. 4:13), but we walk in the Spirit pressing on to make His resurrection our own. So whether it is the loss of someone who has lived a 'full' life or a child who was taken home sooner, our hope is in the powerful resurrection of Jesus that is also ours. Even David found his hope in this when his child died (2 Sam. 12:23).

This resurrection hope reminds us that Jesus Christ is the groom waiting for His bride. God sent Emily for a very specific purpose to be accomplished quickly. He then called her back home. We were blessed to be the receiver of such a gracious gift. The resurrection is our comfort and hope that Emily has heard these words from her Savior, 'I sent you for a short time to accomplish my purpose and you did a great job, "well done my good and faithful servant, now come and receive your reward, enter into my rest forever"' (adapted from Matt. 25:21).

22

The Grief of Children

*The death of a mother is the first
sorrow wept without her.*

AUTHOR UNKNOWN

hildhood is idealized as a time of carefree innocence, little
ones feeling the safety and security of loving parents and a
stable life and thus being free for fun and happiness. Of course,
that ideal is not often realized as life is hard and children face challenges, too. Some wrestle with illness, others with poverty, others
with family instability, and some with more than one of these.
Some also must deal with the death of a loved one, and the closer
that loved one, the greater the grief. The response of children to
the death of a loved one can be different than that of adults, so we
devote a chapter to this unique form of grieving death.

Children are more protected from death than adults are. Recall
our earlier discussion of how our culture walls us off from death
at every opportunity: we move death to hospitals and away from
home. We have even lost our connection to the death of the animals
we eat. In some ways it is healthy for children to experience mild
losses while they are young to introduce them to grief. Not to wish
it upon any one, but the death of a pet can teach lessons about grief
in small doses. As for the death of human beings, the 'natural'
course is for children to first face death when a great-grandparent
or other more distant relative dies. A grandparent's death may
bring this closer to home, depending on how well the child knew
him or her. The tragic death of a classmate or friend may bring

even greater challenges as it breaks down the notion that children certainly have a long time to live.

But no grief hits a child as hard as the death of a parent, as our epigram suggests. As we discuss how children mourn, we will focus on deaths out of season – those that children face that don't fit with the script that says we don't die until we are old.

One of the most common errors in dealing with children who have had a loved one die is separating them from the rituals of grieving. We may keep them from viewing the body, or leave them home from a memorial service. We might fear that going to the gravesite might 'upset' them. Yet unless a child voices strong protests, it is usually best to let him or her be with the family and community for these important rituals. This is another manifestation of our denial of death, and leaving children out leaves them feeling – well, left out. They do well to know they are part of the grieving community. This helps them to deal with their own grief while also helping them to learn the realities of life and death. In some cases, younger children might need an 'escort' or the like for these events if the parents or caregivers are too consumed with grief to attend to the child during these times. A trusted aunt, uncle, or cousin might accompany the child to comfort and explain what is going on should the primary caregiver be too busy with arrangements or too distraught to attend to the child.

Talk with the child about what has happened and is happening. You may need to simplify explanations, but children deserve to know. For example, if Aunt Zelda died of cancer, explain that she had a disease that caused her body not to work right, and this disease was not contagious. Let them know the steps of the funeral service or understand why the family stands beside the body to meet comforters. This can be a teachable time, instructing children not only about the rituals of death and what our faith says about it, but in teaching the child how to grieve in a healthy way.

One particular thing Christians may do wrong is to use euphemisms with young children. To tell a preschooler that 'Grandma has gone to be with Jesus' can be confusing. Think of how much is implicit in that phrase: Jesus being in heaven and grandma going there. For the child who is younger than around six, such a comment might meet with a response such as 'Well, can we go visit her there?' given that the child may not infer that this means an inaccessible and permanent relocation of grandma. It might also be confusing to young children to hear this then see grandma's body, though children seem to get the notion of a 'soul' pretty early in life.

The way information is shared must be sensitive to a child's developmental level. Children younger than 6 or 7 years are more concrete and struggle to grasp abstract notions and ideas, so be thoughtful about how you explain these things. Younger children also process information in a less predictable fashion. Some people worry that children are holding back grief when the situation may be that they grieve intermittently, seeming aloof to the loss one day then sorrowful the next. Children tend to grieve more in episodes than all at once. They also may exhibit more anger and irritability rather than direct sadness.

Continue to follow a child's grief past the memorial service and burial, continue to talk about it. Closed-ended questions like 'Are you doing all right?' won't get much response. Rather, say something like, 'I miss Aunt Zelda sometimes and wonder if you still think about her sometimes.' This gives permission to share grief, and allows the adult to serve as a role model in grieving. Children also do well to hear things like, 'Your mom will be sad some days since your father died, and that is okay. You may see her crying, but God will see her through this, and you will both feel better before too long.' Children may fear grieving behavior as they are unfamiliar with it, so communicating about the process and explaining the behaviors help. Pretending everything is fine rarely will fool a child.

Watch yourself that you don't avoid talking to the child because of your own discomfort. It is generally better for you to face the anxiety of talking with a child about death than to hinder the child's grieving by being quiet. The child, of course, should not be an adult's consolation and bear the brunt of an adult's grief.

However, neither should the child be kept from sharing in the grieving because the adult is avoiding an awkward conversation.

The child is learning to cope with new emotions, and you can aid that by guiding them. Ask if they want to look at pictures of the deceased, or share a memory of a good (or bad) time with that person. If you share a memory to get things started, the child will have a better idea of how this is done. Ask what the child wishes he or she might have told the deceased if there had been an opportunity. If tears follow for either of you, explain to the child that this is fine, and that even Jesus wept (John 11:35), and that was after the death of a loved one.

Children are naturally seekers of meaning, so they will wonder why God would do this to them and to their loved one. Let's be honest: we don't understand, either. Then let them know you don't understand either. Yet, point to the fact that God is trustworthy and that we are limited in our understanding. You might use a metaphor like how the child used to be upset with a parent for not letting him or her play in the street because they were too little to appreciate the danger. God's purposes in death are also wise and we are just not able to understand them.

Communicate to the church community not to treat a bereaved child as if he or she had the plague. Speak to the child, let him or her know you are sad too and are praying for the family. Teachers in the child's Sunday School class can use these times to teach the other children to be aware of the grief and not exclude the child due to feeling uncomfortable about what to say or do. If another child in the community has been through a similar loss, connecting the two would be a ministry to both.

If the deceased was the caregiver for a child, leaving only one parent, then a legitimate question the child might have is who will take care of me if the other person dies? One of the toughest things for the child to adjust to is the new unpredictability in his or her world. I think we all identify with this, but it may be more pronounced for children. So answers to such questions are helpful. The child will also benefit from routines that are predictable as the family may struggle to find a new rhythm of life. The child's irritability may be frustrating, but calm, fair consequences delivered with empathy help ground the child as he or she learns to manage the new feelings that come after a loss.

Even such painful events as the death of loved ones can be used to God's glory as they deepen our faith and cause us to cast our hope on God as we realize our lack of control. Children, too, can learn these lessons as they watch us grieve and learn to mourn themselves, for 'blessed are those who mourn, for they will be comforted' (Matt. 5:4). Let us pray for special grace for children who mourn that they receive an abundance of comfort.

Part V

After a Loved One Dies

Introduction

You may have been surprised by the death. You may have been relieved to know the person you loved was through with a long and painful illness. But now there is no denying the death. There is no more hoping for a miracle cure. God has taken your loved one away.

For all the hopeful platitudes that Christians like to cite to someone who is mourning, the truth is that it is a deeply sorrowful time. Yes, there is hope in Christ if the loved one was a believer. But that does not change that this hurts. Grieving a death and adjusting to live a new life without the beloved takes time, no matter how deep your faith.

You will mourn your loss. You will feel the pain. The only question is how will you mourn? Some ways are more helpful than others, and bitter mourning can lead to depression, anger, and a more distant relationship with God. Toward the goal of mourning that is spiritually healthy, I offer the last few chapters of our meditations.

23
Mourning Well

*Christians sometimes think that we are not supposed to
grieve, because our faith and theology provide us with
confidence about heaven and eternal life. But while 1
Thessalonians 4:13 says that we are not to grieve as those
who have no hope, we grieve nevertheless. Those without
hope grieve in one way; those with hope grieve in another.*

ALBERT Y. HSU[1]

One thing I remember from my grandfather's funeral was
my grandmother coaching the family not to cry or say
things that might lead to tears. Emotions were to be contained
for who knew what might happen should sadness and grief be
given free rein. The funeral director provided an appropriate
place for the family, shielded from the view of onlookers, so
that if we did express feelings, we would not have the 'shame' of
others seeing us. As if it were a bad thing to mourn the loss of
such a wonderful person as my grandfather!

Fast forward a few years to the death of my best friend's
father. He and his family are African-American and the service
to honor his memory was held at an African-American church.
I was startled when the family actually processed into the
room to sit in the front, with his sister wailing in grief. I was
in shock. Feelings were expressed without restraint, though as

---

1. *Grieving a Suicide: A Loved One's Search for Comfort, Answers & Hope*
(Downers Grove, IL: InterVarsity), 2002; p. 41.

the service progressed, mourning was turned to joy as the shift was made to considering the eternal bliss into which this man had entered.

Partly these differences are cultural. Western cultures, British and American, promote holding in feelings of grief; other cultures promote expression. Yet, Westerners may justify such stoicism by our theology. We may argue that given the prospect of eternal life, we should rejoice for those who die and to be sad is selfish.

Those things are, to an extent, true. We are to live in hope of resurrection, and there is a sense in which we rejoice in the 'homegoing' of those who die in Christ. But not to mourn at all? I'm not so sure we can conclude that from looking at the Bible.

Consider these touching verses:

> *When Jesus saw her weeping, and the Jews who had come with her also weeping, he was deeply moved in his spirit and greatly troubled. And he said, 'Where have you laid him?' They said to him, 'Lord, come and see.' Jesus wept. So the Jews said, 'See how he loved him!'* (John 11:33-36)

The context, of course, is the death of Lazarus and the sadness of a family to which Jesus was particularly close. Yet, Jesus does not rebuke Mary or the funeral party for being tearful. He actually is moved to tears Himself. One might argue that this was because of their faithlessness, but the better understanding is that He came alongside them in their suffering – even as He acted to end it. Jesus was, after all, as Isaiah 53 tells us, 'a man of sorrows and acquainted with grief.' The scene seems to recall the funeral of my friend's father more than that of my grandfather.

Mourning is not overlooked in Scripture, and death and loss were constant companions of the psalmist David who endured the death of his beloved friend Jonathan, several children, and others that he cared deeply for. If you review his numerous laments in the Psalms, you would almost take him to be a complainer. Yet he was not shy to bring his hurt to God. His prayers about death included:

Remember how short my time is!
  For what vanity you have created all the
    children of man!
What man can live and never see death?
  Who can deliver his soul from the power of
    Sheol?   (Ps. 89:47-48)

We could easily go on to show the grief expressed by Moses (e.g., Ps. 90) and others, but I think for our purposes we can establish that mourning is something that is acceptable to God and demonstrated in the Bible, not something to be shunned as either lacking faith or for fear of losing emotional control.

Remember, we are not to mourn as those who have no hope (as noted in the epigraph above). The exception to this, of course, is the exceptionally profound sorrow of the death of a loved one who was not a Christian. While we often try to figure some hope that such loved ones are somehow Christ's sheep, we know there is exceptional grief in this type of loss. There is no real consolation for this. We hope and pray that this moves others who knew the person to draw near to Christ, or challenges believers to be more active in evangelism, for God wondrously works all things together for good (Rom. 8:28) – even if we have no idea how that will look.

But there is still sorrow for saints who depart. Yes, we rejoice that they are made pure, are no longer in pain, are in the presence of God, and know a joy they never experienced on earth. Our mourning is not for them, but for our loss. We bewail the loss of companionship, the end of good memories being made, the grandchildren that won't know the loved one, the hardships of losing a source of support. But most of all, we mourn the piece of our lives that will not be replaced. God is sufficient and gracious, but such platitudes don't make experiencing loss painless.

There are not many more profound stories of grief and loss than of the great Saint Augustine as he describes in his classic *Confessions*. His mother prayed diligently for many years that he would come to follow Christ. After he was converted to Christ, Augustine and his mother, Monica, shared some special spiritual experience though he doesn't share the details. Not long after this, Monica dies and Augustine makes clear in his spiritual autobiography that he wept over her – even in a culture that viewed that as unseemly.

A few suggestions about mourning well are in order.

First, please don't try to conform your grief to some idea of what it 'ought' to look like. We are all different and mourn differently. No one is to say how long you should grieve, or how intently, or whether silently or with wailing. No one should tell you to go through certain stages as though there is a prescribed way to mourn a loss. Grief does not have to conform to the number of days your job gives you off for a funeral. Nor do you have to lament in the ways your friends may suggest. Just grieve – in your own way.

Don't be shy to be honest with God. David and others were honest in expressing their burdens to God in the laments of Scripture. God can take it, I'm sure. Be slow to ask God to take away your sorrow and spend more time letting Him be with you in your sorrow. The Holy Spirit is a Comforter, not an anesthetic. God will walk with you through the valley of the shadow of death, but He doesn't usually just fix our pain and make it go away. Losing a loved one hurts, and there are no short cuts to that – even for Christians.

Mourn when you are alone. Resist the temptation just to keep busy. As often as you need to, seek out a quiet place and talk with God. Again, that is not to prescribe crying or 'analyzing' your loss. Needs will vary among the bereaved. However you spend the time, do make a time and place for it and savor sharing your burden with God when no one else sees.

Yet, don't mourn only by yourself. My grandmother meant well by exhorting us not to stir up sadness, but she deprived herself and others of the comfort God intends us to receive through family and friends. How can others bear our burdens if we don't give them a chance? God intends for us to console one another, so try not to neglect this source of comfort. War veterans share a peculiar closeness even after combat has ceased. Why? Bonds of intimacy increase when stresses are shared. Mourning your loss with loved ones draws you closer to them.

Mourn with your church family. Involve your pastors and church leaders in the process. Welcome food, gifts, and visits from your brothers and sisters in Christ. Rise above the false piety that pretends you don't need their help or support. A closer look at that is likely to reveal more pride than spiritual maturity. Sure, you may need to set limits if the outreach to you is overwhelming, but let others serve God by serving you. I was astounded once when I heard Joni Eareckson-Tada, who is a quadriplegic, speak. Almost utterly helpless, she is dependent on others for virtually all of her self-care. Her response: God uses her handicap to provide opportunity to serve for others who desire to serve. Similarly, your grief is an occasion for others to honor you and God by their ministry to you. Don't shun the grace God offers through His church.

If you have children, mourn with them. Some of my earliest work with grief was leading groups for children whose parents had died while the children were still young. I learned that efforts to 'protect' them from sadness could hurt them. Most always they want to go to the funeral or pay last respects to a loved one. While they mourn differently than adults in many ways, they benefit from seeing adults mourn and then move toward recovering from the loss. In this they can learn important lessons about life. I'm not saying turn to children as your primary supporters or care-givers, overburdening them with your grief. But conversely, don't try to hide your grief from them completely. They generally know you are sad and may think things are worse than they are.

Your feeling of loss and sadness will come and go, wax better then worse. But there is no need to make it fit a particular course or time frame. Reminisce, sort through old pictures, reflect on things and places that remind you of time spent with the loved one. Tell stories, laugh, weep, and even feel the anxiety and uncertainties that the loss may bring to your life. God will sustain you through His Spirit and His family.

❧ PRAYER ❦

God, grant us grace to mourn well, to be honest with You yet to receive the comfort of Your Holy Spirit as we adjust to life without the one we loved.

24
Remembering Well

The song is ended, but the melody lingers on...

IRVING BERLIN

You walk away from the gravesite. The days since your loved one died have been few but busy. Friends and family have been together, and getting through the memorial service and burial have kept people focused. Now the really hard part: back to normal life. Yet, life will not be normal anymore. You begin a new life without your beloved. This new life will be marked by many changes. In this chapter we will focus on the memories that will accompany you the rest of your life. In the next we will consider the other changes that may come to your life.

Breaking these reflections into separate chapters may make each aspect of grief seem separate and isolated, but in truth they all weave together in a whole. The mourning process we looked at does not magically end at the burial, or at any designated point after the death. Don't believe those that tell you that time will heal this wound. Death is not a wound; it is a loss. 'Healing' is an idea that comes from the medicalization of death, and assumes anything that is painful can be 'healed' in time. Mourning will relent, but will not disappear. Like the echoes of the melody of a song, it will linger in your mind – forever.

If we will remember our lost loved one, then let us remember well. Memories have often been called bittersweet. That makes sense, too, for we recall good times with fondness only for this to slide into melancholy as we realize those times will never come again. So many things now will remind you of the loved one. If you lived with the person who died, every part of the house will teem with things that trigger memories. There will be many tears, and that is fine. God gave us tears for many reasons, and this would be one of them. Embrace your memories and your tears. The New Testament at no point says you will not suffer in this life; in fact, it assumes you will suffer. Since death is the consequence of sin, it is not surprising that it would bring suffering.

Value your memories, and don't try to avoid them. Sure, you might go too far and obsess about the days when your loved one was alive, but generally it is best to entertain memories, even if they are unpleasant. The good news is that over time the joy of the memories becomes stronger than the bitterness they may bring now.

Let us first address the memories that may cause you particular distress. Maybe your beloved died with there being tension between the two of you. You might have held a grudge against that person, or vice versa, and you did not manage to be reconciled on it before it was too late. You can know with confidence that your loved one would have forgiven you. How can I say that? Because if your loved one is with Christ, he or she knows the full joy of being forgiven and will forgive you in the same way Christ forgives. Even if the person was not a Christian, we learned from the story of Lazarus that the pangs of hell made the rich man long for peace for loved ones left behind (Luke 16:27-28).

If you are the one who held the grudge, forgiveness is still possible. Pray for grace to forgive the loved one, knowing how our Lord's model prayer calls us to this. As you are more aware of mortality, the grievance should shrivel in its significance and make room for forgiveness.

You may have other regrets. Maybe you feel you did not do all you could to help your loved one during his or her last days. Or maybe you were not the spouse/child/sibling or whatever that you should have been. Just as you are helpless to 'make it up' to God for your sins and shortcomings, you are helpless to compensate for these. Some of your regrets may be exaggerated by your grief, but either way, lay your regrets at the foot of the cross, knowing that you are forgiven. Some of your regrets may be for things that really were not sins. It is easy to feel guilt for not doing something you could not do. You could not always be there, or personally make a person happy. The key is that, before God, you did what you could do – even if it was not enough.

Putting aside the memories of your shortcomings or tensions you had with the deceased, we move to discuss more positive ways of remembering. In the weeks and months following a loss, it might be helpful to put together the story of your relationship with the lost loved one. In free moments, try to think through the story of your relationship. Begin with your earliest memory, or the time you met. If not a family member, recall what attracted you to the loved one. What did you do together? How did your relationship change and grow over time? What are your best memories together? What things did you enjoy doing together? What moments of closeness to God did you share? Were there moments of tension and disagreement? How were these resolved (or not)? What were the places you remember sharing – a home if you lived with the person, or the house where you visited the person? Did you go on any trips or outings that are particularly meaningful? Were there times where the person cared for you in a special way – during an illness, or after the birth of a child? What are lessons you learned from the person? What character qualities or fruit of the Spirit were manifest in his or her life? How did the relationship change near the end, or was the end so sudden you did not get to say final farewells? What stories did you share with others? Might you share these memories with them? Thank God for each memory you have and consider how God was present in it.

You may just think through this mentally as a way to organize the story of your relationship and reflect on what your special person meant to you. You might find photos and make a collage, or edit a video from footage taken of the special person.

There may be pain in doing all of this, knowing that the story of the relationship has come to an end – at least for now. Yet, the treasures of your memories with your beloved can be gathered as a bouquet that is sweet. You may find that by stepping into remembering that the sting of loss recedes as the peace and joy of your memories takes center stage. In this process you may begin to feel the beginning of a sense of letting go of the relationship. No, you do not release the memories, but move to a place where you accept that God has taken your loved one home, and your life will move on without the person's physical presence.

If you have tokens of affection from the loved one, like gifts, cards, or letters, you might round these up and make them into a keepsake. If you lived with the person, you might choose certain objects that are especially meaningful and determine to keep them for memory's sake. If you have lots of things (clothing, books, collectibles) of the person, consider sharing some of these with others who might value a memento of the person, or with others who could use them, thus extending the ministry of the lost loved one into the lives of others. While tokens of memory are wonderful, you may not want to keep the house too much the way it was as this may hinder you from letting go and moving on into the next phase of your life.

Certain cues will make memories and emotions more vivid. Places you went with the loved one, or songs you enjoyed, or foods you enjoyed together will pique your mind and emotions. Of course, dates will also stir memories and some sadness. Wedding anniversaries and birthdays are common triggers for grieving, though likely the most powerful one is the anniversary of the death. Often a few days of sadness come at the first anniversary in particular, but also in later ones to a lesser extent. Feel the sadness of loss and missing the person at these times, but also turn the sadness of now into an occasion to celebrate the many good times you shared.

My father died ten years ago tomorrow. At about the time of evening I am writing this I unknowingly said goodbye to him for the last time. A decade later, these memories are still vivid, and I believe this is quite normal. Yet I take occasion from this cue to reflect on the wonderful life my father led, and how he served Jesus so very well. A plant from his funeral adorns my office and also serves as a reminder of his passing. This new 'life' in my life is a reminder that he is still alive and oh so very happy in the presence of his Lord. Yes, I miss him, but would not want to have him back if it meant taking him away from heavenly bliss!

Life must continue, but the memories echo in the mind. In a world that says intense pleasure is what makes life worth living, the Christian can learn that bittersweet memories can bring a joy and peace the world cannot know.

❧ PRAYER ❦
Heavenly Father, we thank You for the gift of memory
that keeps a loved one alive in our minds, and speaks
to us of our hope in Christ.

25

Temptations and Virtues for Those Who Grieve

We bereaved are not alone. We belong to the largest company in all the world – the company of those who have known suffering.

HELEN KELLER[1]

The death of a loved one poses many challenges for those who remain behind. Depending on your relationship to the deceased, the challenges vary. Mourning is characteristic of all who have lost someone, but the impact on daily life varies greatly. A widow will feel the loss profoundly as she lives in a place where reminders of her loss are everywhere. An adult child may be less directly affected, but wrestle with facing decisions in life without consulting a lost parent. Finances may change, too. An early death may lead to financial struggles for those who survive, while in some cases an inheritance eases financial pressure. There are, then, a variety of challenges that may be encountered that merit some reflection.

In our section addressed to the individual who is dying, there is a chapter based on Allen Verhey's excellent book describing and reflecting on the ancient Christian 'art of dying'[2]. Based on a fifteenth Century Christian book, he shares some of the

---

1. From *Peace at Eventide*, 1929, last accessed 2/16/2017 at https://archive.org/stream/peaceateventide00hele/peaceateventide00hele_djvu.txt.

2. Verhey, *The Christian Art of Dying: Learning from Jesus* (Grand Rapids, MI: Eerdmans), 2011.

temptations the dying person faces, and the virtues that empower the person to overcome them. In this chapter I review this list again, but now with focus on how these apply to the person who grieves the death of a loved one.

Losing versus Keeping Faith

The loss of a beloved person sometimes reveals how much we depended on that person in ways we didn't realize. Even as we grieve the death, we now face life with lowered emotional support, more burden as we pick up additional responsibilities, and possibly financial hardships. Activities enjoyed together are either avoided or done alone. Grief quickly slips into loneliness. This may be complicated by having held out so much hope for the person to recover that we are not as prepared for the actual death. We may be angry with God for not answering our prayers to lengthen the life of the loved one. Through all of this, it is easy to be tempted to lose faith. We did not want that person to die, and we don't want to go through this painful time of grief, loneliness, and change. God may indeed seem to have forsaken us.

But of course we know he has not. Satan may buffet our faith but God will not forsake us. As mentioned earlier, we must resist the enemy's efforts to weaken our faith (1 Pet. 5:9). But how to do this? First, be honest with God. Lament and express your anxieties, doubts, and loneliness. Don't be a Christian who paints on a happy face and in so doing keeps those who might support you at a distance.

Also consider the wisdom of Psalm 23:4. We walk through the valley of the shadow of death. Sure it is a valley, but it is also a walk. It is not a moment in time that we grieve, but we journey through grief. It is a difficult time, but we must continue to walk with our good Shepherd until we have passed through. In the meantime, His rod and staff comfort us. The rod was used by a shepherd to ward off wolves and other would-be attackers, and so our Shepherd will defend us against Satan's attacks. The shepherd's staff had a hook to pull the straying sheep back into the path, thus protecting it from dangers. God will be merciful with us as we tend to stray from the path in this treacherous part of life's journey. While we will always grieve our lost loved one, we will move past the valley to a new phase of life. We do well, then, to trust the Shepherd who knows the terrain well and will see us through safely.

One reason we may lose hope as we go through mourning is that we forget how much a part of the Christian life suffering plays. Popular Christian media may have distorted our understanding of Scripture and misled us to believe that the Christian life is always pleasure. We have touched on this several times and I won't belabor the fact that the New Testament teaches us to expect suffering, other than to remind us that we follow a Savior who was 'a man of sorrows and acquainted with grief' (Isa. 53:3). With this in mind, reread the Helen Keller quote above.

Despair versus Hope

The natural pain of loss can be complicated if we listen to voices that would complicate our grief. You may feel guilty that you did not do enough for the loved one in life or in death. You may feel God is punishing you or deserting you. You may push others away, feeling they don't understand. You may be angry with doctors or other family members who did not do their share. There are many thoughts and feelings that may creep into your grief that might lead you to despair. See these for what they are: distractions from hoping in God. Pray that God will comfort you, certainly. But know that He uses suffering and change to cause us to hope in Him. See the larger purpose of God that has brought the loved one into His presence, and that He intends to mature your faith to see how He is with us in our adversities.

Join with the Sons of Korah in Psalm 42 as they lamented how they thirsted for God. In hard times others were questioning God, leading to their tears being their food day and night (v. 3). The refrain they turned to in their misery was, 'Why are you cast down, O my soul, and why are you in turmoil within me? Hope in God, for I shall again praise him, my salvation and my God' (vv. 5 and 11).

Impatience versus Patience/Love

Grief is not a brief thing. It lingers and continues to reappear even after it has subsided. We want to feel better – and soon. So, there is the temptation to become impatient with the process. It is similar with regards to life changes that follow bereavement – they are ongoing and not just brief. We are tempted to complain, wanting relief now. But as Christians we have the Holy Spirit whose fruit is patience (Gal. 5:22). For us, hardships are the soil in which spiritual growth occurs.

Consider Paul's wisdom in Romans 5:3-5: 'Not only that, but we rejoice in our sufferings, knowing that suffering produces endurance, and endurance produces character, and character produces hope, and hope does not put us to shame, because God's love has been poured into our hearts through the Holy Spirit who has been given to us.' Patience is tied to love, for we can be patient as we trust that all He does flows from His love for us. It is more than we can grasp, but He loves us more than we love ourselves.

I remember a dreadful day from my childhood, when after repeated trips to the doctor, my parents decided to put me in hospital. I begged and pleaded with them not to do this – even promising I'd get better as I recall. They did not relent, and put me in hospital where I had a spinal tap and was given numerous injections in my derriere to the point that I could not even sit without hurting. Child abuse? Hardly. I had spinal meningitis and these painful procedures saved my life. More mature now, I am very grateful to them for loving me more than I loved myself. If my parents understood better than I did, consider how much more God knows what He is doing when He brings suffering into our lives.

Pride versus humility

How can one be tempted to pride in the midst of grief? You feel helpless and out of control as you have lost someone you did not want to lose. This very fact can lead to pride in an effort to compensate for feeling vulnerable. You may mask your sorrow and minimize how much you are struggling when others ask. Even as you wear yourself out trying to adjust to life without the loved one, you may reject offers of help from family, friends, and the church community. This may even be justified by thoughts like, 'They've done enough already.' You may even unwisely refuse the invitation to move into a family member's home or accept help to keep your present house up.

But behind this may lie pride, the desire to show you can tough it out and do it on your own. Sure, it will take courage and perseverance to move through your grief, but we are called, after all, to 'bear one another's burdens' (Gal. 6:2). Don't let pride deprive those around you of the opportunity to obey Paul's words.

There is much room for humility. Who among us knows completely how to walk through grief? You have not experienced this loss before, so how can you know how to navigate it? And who knows the mind of God well enough to explain why this was the time for your loved one to die? None of us knows this. We humbly yield to a God who is faithful to us, and admit to those around us that we are inadequate for the task.

Avarice versus 'Letting Go'

For the dying person, the longing to cling to worldly goods can reveal avarice in the heart. The love of possessions may also show up in the life of a mourner. You may grieve the loss of income in your home due to the death of a loved one, or feel overwhelmed by the medical bills you face. You may resist the need to move to smaller, less comfortable living arrangements. You may resent no longer being able to do some things you could do before. Faith can be tested by these financial struggles also.

For some, the temptation will be in the opposite direction. You may guiltily feel a hidden shudder of excitement at the inheritance you receive. Not that you should not enjoy things that the deceased may have labored hard to leave to you, but easily money and goods can become idols.

Rather, the Christian will keep material things in their proper place. Death reminds us that life is merely the prelude to eternity, and earthly goods merely a resource to sustain us in our journey to eternity. Sing with Martin Luther, 'let goods and kindred go', and be resigned to serve God and be sheltered by this Mighty Fortress.

26

Living in Light of Loss

But when David saw that his servants were whispering
together, David understood that the child was dead.
And David said to his servants, 'Is the child dead?'
They said, 'He is dead.' Then David arose from the
earth and washed and anointed himself and changed
his clothes. And he went into the house of the Lord
and worshiped. He then went to his own house. And
when he asked, they set food before him, and he ate.

2 Samuel 12:19-20

When the memorial service is over and everyone goes home, those who mourn return to a new life – one with changes because of the hole in life without the beloved. We have focused on grieving already, so in this chapter we turn to consider making needed changes in life after the death of the loved one. This will look different for different people, of course, as the departed might have had varying roles in the lives of different mourners: from a spouse who now must learn to live as a widow, to a sibling who loses a conversation partner and source of encouragement, to an adult child who loses an advisor, to a Christian brother or sister who loses a friend to spend time with and walk with through life. As a result, the reader may need to select aspects of what follows as they apply to his or her particular situation.

It is important to note in what follows that it is all done in the context of grief. Life changes are stressful even under good circumstances, like moving to a new city to take a dream job.

But adjusting to life after loss is more challenging because it happens with the backdrop of mourning and grief. You may also be mentally, emotionally, physically, and spiritually exhausted if you have walked through a long period of caregiving prior to the death. All of this means fatigue and mental fuzziness may make adjustments more challenging. The frayed emotions of one who has suffered loss may leave fewer resources for facing the anxieties and uncertainties associated with life transitions. Be patient with yourself, and be generous in accepting help and counsel from those around you as you go through this period of time.

The Bible passage above may be a strange one for this chapter and there is little in Scripture that precisely tells what to do after a loved one dies. Recall that Jesus basically arranged for John to be his mother's protector and provider (John 19:26-27), making clear the importance of having someone to watch over mourners. It also appears from the text that Mary had already been widowed, so she was in quite a vulnerable position.

The passage about David comes as he ends a period of spiritual watching and praying as his illegitimate son (from his adultery with Bathsheba) dies. His soul sorrow was so intense that his advisors even feared breaking the news of the death to him. They were startled when David handled it the way he did. He cleaned himself up and refreshed himself, worshiped God, then returned home to eat.

David's situation was rife with guilt and remorse, and he almost certainly was aware that the child's death was punishment for his sin. Your process will not likely have these complications in it, but that David acted as he did in his dire circumstances suggests maybe those who face less complicated ones can learn something.

The primary point from this scene is that once the death had occurred, David accepted God's decision in taking the loved one and stepped into his life after his sordid doings. God had called David to be king long before this had happened, and God had known even then how His servant would fail. We learn from this that God was also not caught off guard by your loss and His calling on your life had this time built into it. Maybe part of David's worship was to praise God's sovereignty and ask for grace to move forward after the loss. This seems a wonderful way to approach God in your situation, too.

There are a variety of changes that may ensue in your life, and we will start from the most external and move to the internal ones.

External changes may include most specifically housing. Particularly older widows or widowers may now face a decision about where to live if they are unable to manage alone. Or, they might consider having caregivers come into the home if that is possible. Other changes might be moving to a smaller home or an apartment, or to a city near or with a family member. Part of the decision may come from health and ability. Are you able to live alone physically? The other factor might be the inability to stay in a living space due to lost income after the loved one's death. Moreover, a move might mean having to sell or give away some furnishings from your home, another loss that, though minor, adds to the burden.

Such changes are particularly hard for older adults who find comfort in the familiarity of their homes, apartments, or flats. To move away is to lose some sense of security and even safety. It is understandable that this is a difficult thing to do.

Here is where it is important to look to God for your security and seek the virtue of faith. More changes are hard, but God will walk through them with you. Seek God's wisdom about these decisions and be courageous. It may be easier to make changes now, while life is upended, than to have to do it later on after life has stabilized.

Just a quick word to family who might be in the position of inviting a loved one into your home after a death. While it can be inconvenient and sometimes frustrating, there is great satisfaction in showing godly hospitality when someone is in need. Be understanding of how this might be to the guest you consider entertaining. Caring for widows and widowers is a central ministry of Christ's body (e.g., Deut. 26:12), and of one's family.

Other financial changes may ensue, and there may need to be some tense family discussions at this point. Sadly, the dividing of an inheritance has caused many family rifts. Here the wisdom of

Romans 12:18 is central: 'If possible, so far as it depends on you, live peaceably with all.' Harmony in a family is worth far more than riches.

Changes in one's relationships may also follow the death of a loved one. You may no longer have transportation to get to church or other places where you meet with others. If you lost a spouse, activities with other couples may not be an option as it had been. For other family members, there may be some sacrifice of time with others to be with a parent, aunt, or uncle who was widowed. You may have lost a person with whom you shared your struggles in life or to whom you looked for guidance and wisdom.

I believe these matters are more subtle than we may realize. Building new relationships takes emotional energy, and there is not an abundance of that when one is grieving. This may leave you with an inclination to stay at home and not reach out to others. Doing what is more comfortable in the short run may hinder your building the relationships you need in the long run. Seek God's grace to reach out. Put yourself around other people at church and in other social activities. Cultivate new friendships. You may have to take the initiative, but not only will new relationships fill a void for you, you will have an impact on the other people. Everyone wins.

Just a few words now on emotional changes. Grief is a very powerful emotion, or maybe better, set of emotions. For a while you may feel down, discouraged, lost and lonely most of the time. This is the time for lament as we discussed earlier. As the days slowly pass, you will not feel quite as bad and begin to experience periods of a new normalcy. Of course, each person's journey will be different, but most often things improve. If you don't begin to feel better after a couple of months, reach out to a pastor or trusted counselor to seek assistance.

Even as a more balanced mood emerges, there will still be periods of sadness. Some will be triggered by a sight, sound, or even smell that is associated with the loved one. Other times sadness will just appear. Anniversaries and special dates (birthdays, for example) may also stir the embers of your grief. This is natural, and don't try to fight them or avoid them. Lay them before your

Lord. Savor the bitter sweetness of the memories. Being with others and sharing these emotions with trusted loved ones also helps to smooth the ups and downs of the emotional rollercoaster.

Spiritual changes are also likely to occur. A loss can draw you closer to God or push you away. You may feel anger toward Him for not sparing the life of your beloved, and He can handle your expressing that. You may feel God has forsaken you because of the profundity of your sorrow. You may also be hurt that your family, friends, and/or church have not rallied to support you as much as you wished, and see God's people as having failed you. These are very understandable feelings in the midst of grief.

Yet, I exhort you to look above the dark valley to the light above. God walks with us through it, but He does not avoid it. Seek fellowship with the God who sent His Son to suffer for you. Bathe in the awareness that He is with you, but be patient with the pain. God grows us through difficulties, and to become angry with Him because of them is like being angry with a personal trainer who pushes you to do harder exercises to improve your fitness.

The spiritual goal in this is for loss to bring you to an even closer walk with God. You will learn to depend on Him more than ever after losing a loved one. You will find the intimacy that comes from walking through hard times with your Lord and with His people. I am reminded of the comradery of those who served together in wars. Shared hardships bring intimacy. In the long run your spiritual growth will bring you to an even greater gratitude to God and the hope you have in Christ – and thus to a place of greater fruitfulness for His Kingdom.

❧ PRAYER ❧
God, guide us through these hard times to teach us that You go with us in our pain and will lead us into Your glory.

27

The Poignant Pain at the Death of an Unbeliever

Most men eddy about
here and there – eat and drink,
chatter and love and hate,
gather and squander, are raised
aloft, and hurl'd in the dust,
striving blindly, achieving nothing;
– And then they die.

MATTHEW ARNOLD[1]

The lines above are a sad commentary on the life of a person without Christ – a life spent with much done but nothing accomplished in light of eternity. Maybe such a one leaves the world a better place in some ways, but that does not buy immortality nor meaning at death. And dying apart from Christ has eternal consequences, if we believe the words of Jesus.

We enter into a discussion that frankly is about the most daunting chapter for me to write. How does a Christian grieve the death of a loved one who did not profess Christ? Time and again in our discussions we're pointed back to the hope we have in Christ for eternal life, and how though we grieve, we do 'not grieve as others do who have no hope' (1 Thess. 4:13). But there is no hope for those

---

1. From the poem, *Rugby Chapel*, last accessed 2/16/2017 at https://www. poetryfoundation.org/poems-and-poets/poems/detail/43601.

who die in their sins. As heart wrenching as death is in the best of circumstances, this sorrow is multiplied when we consider the fate of a loved one who died outside of Christ. Maybe for some we have some glimmer of hope that they belonged to Christ, but in many cases we are relatively certain that they did not.

A theme in our reflections has been the denial of death we have in the modern West. We keep occupied and entertained in part to avoid considering the reality that we are mortal. Christians may also be guilty of denying the reality of hell and the fate of those who die in their sin. Hell is more often an item we check off a list of points of doctrine than an actual place that we have given much thought to. The old hell-fire and brimstone sermons may have been too coercive, but now the topic is more likely swept under the carpet in our pulpits and churches. The result is that when we actually contemplate the fate of a person without Christ, we may find a tension between what we believe theologically and how that plays out in our lives.

Let us begin with the simple fact that Jesus taught about hell. He spoke of it more often than He spoke of heaven, which is a sobering thought. One of the most familiar treatments is Jesus's story of the rich man and Lazarus in Luke 16:19-31. The rich man is seen in misery, longing for his thirst to be quenched, then for his loved ones to be warned of their fate. Jesus directly warns us to fear hell in Matthew 10:28, saying, 'And do not fear those who kill the body but cannot kill the soul. Rather fear him who can destroy both soul and body in hell.' We will not go into detail about the miseries of those who go there, but suffice it to say this is not a fate we wish on anyone.

Yet now here you are, reflecting on the fact that the loved one you lost is sharing in the rich man's fate. The grief of the loss is without the hope of resurrection. This is a devastating situation. The sorrow and grief is without measure.

This is where the question may come up, 'But how is this even fair?' How can less than one-hundred years of living in sin be fairly compensated by an eternity of suffering? God may appear to be mean and petty, using his infinite power to punish those who defy Him. I am unsure whether anything I might say at this point can answer these hard questions, yet I will venture a few thoughts just in case.

Part of our problem is that we tend to judge sin by our own experience. We know our frailties and while others may be worse, they, too, are human and fail. Sin is bad, but it is a challenge to see it as God sees it. God is absolutely holy, and also just. As holy, He cannot allow sin before Him. As we know, only a few germs following a surgery can cause a serious infection. So God does not tolerate anything that is not holy.

This standard was evident with Adam and Eve in the garden: their seemingly small sin of eating a piece of fruit in reality reflected their rejection of His authority and wisdom and led not only to their death and being cast out of the garden, but to a sinful nature characterizing all who came from their union. Sin is worse than we think, and that is because we view it through human, rather than divine, eyes.

Of course, the good news is that God's grace is greater than our sin. The Second Adam, Jesus, died. Consider that God could not just say 'Oh, never mind. Human beings are sinful. I'll just overlook it.' Not at all. It required the death of the Second Person of the Trinity – the death of One with no sin at all. Our sin caused His death. But as fearsome as God's wrath is, His grace is more amazing as Jesus's death atoned for the sins of all who would ever call on His Name. The potency of the sacrifice overcame the blight of sin.

Once again in considering death we face the *mysterium tremendum*, the terrible mystery of God. Since we can only grasp the smallest idea of what His holiness is like, we cannot grasp the severity of the evil of sin that opposes it. Nor can we grasp why God would allow anyone to die in sin. Whatever your view on predestination, God did not set up a failsafe plan so that no one dies in sin. Whether by God's foreordination or by a person's free will, some do not come to know Christ. We are simply incapable of understanding this. Our frustration at God's justice merely reflects how little we understand.

So what might be the comfort? It cannot be found in a 'happy ending' for the one you lost, but only in a grander scheme of this death somehow vindicating the justice of God. Abraham challenged God's threat to destroy Sodom with the question, 'Far be it from you to do such a thing, to put the righteous to death with the wicked, so that the righteous fare as the wicked! Far be that from you! Shall not the Judge of all the earth do what is just?' (Gen. 18:25), and learned that the answer is 'yes'. God is the Judge, and 'right' is more than we can grasp right now.

The hope we have, then, is in the promise that when we, too, are without sin before God, He will wipe away every tear from our eyes (Rev. 21:4), including those shed for loved ones lost forever. Somehow, when we understand holiness more fully, we will find comfort in how God has meted out justice.

Is the sentence of those dying in their sins fair? We have to say it is, or God is unjust. Throughout history, many parents have watched as their children were executed for crimes they had committed. Horribly sad, yet deserved. Jesus did not do anything for the thief on the cross who chided Him, letting him suffer the fate that he merited. Fair as it may be, we mourn, and hope that we will know comfort when we are with Jesus someday.

For all of us, these thoughts challenge us to speak more openly about the Gospel, calling others to repentance. The rich man in hell pleads for God to send Lazarus to his family to warn them of the fate to come (Luke 16:28). We might imagine your lost loved one making the same request of us. This might be at least one good thing to come from this loss. Being awakened to the seriousness of life and death for eternity, let us resolve to speak of God's forgiveness and the hope of eternal life to all that God brings across our paths.

❧ PRAYER ❧

God, in Your mercy grant us faith to trust You
in these sobering matters, and challenge us to be
obedient to Your call to preach the Gospel and
make disciples (Matt. 28:19-20).

28

The Role of the Grieving Christian Community

Religion that is pure and undefiled before God the Father is this: to visit orphans and widows in their affliction, and to keep oneself unstained from the world.

JAMES 1:27

James makes the Christian life pretty simple by summarizing pure and undefiled religion as three things. Purity of life is not surprising, as all Christians long to be more like Jesus who was sinless and pure. To do that we have to fight to avoid being stained by the world.

Maybe more surprising is that the other two of the three relate to caring for those who have lost family. Orphans are those whose parents have died and widows have lost a husband. Moreover, this assumes that those who are thus bereaved are in affliction. That is, life that brings pain and suffering in unique ways. In Bible times there were no social welfare programs to help those without family to care for them. Women had limited opportunity for earning, and children even less. So, a theme of both testaments is that those who love and serve God will focus ministry on these groups in particular.

It is thus at the heart of the mission of the church to care for those who have experienced the death of family members, and by extension, to all who mourn. I even wonder if it is not pushing the text too much to say that when Jesus promised that mourners would be blessed with comfort (Matt. 5:4) that He expected to use His church as a means for that grace.

The church and Christian community tend to do a reasonably good job during the days after a death. We dispatch our pastors and church leaders to comfort and to lead the memorial services. We send flowers and food to the family. We visit the family to show our support, and we pray for those who grieve.

But the affliction of the widow and orphan, and others who lose loved ones, is not just short-term. We have already seen how our media-saturated culture lends itself to attending to a crisis for a few days only to have it shoved into the background by a newer story. This leaves us responding to a crisis but not having sustained care for more chronic needs. We have noted how the worst time for mourners is often after the funeral when they go home to a new and different world as their comforters return to their old worlds.

We will then focus in these last few pages on ways the church and Christians can minister to mourners over the long term, when the post-loss afflictions set in and awareness of the need often fades.

Church leadership might consider regular follow-up visits to the family who grieve. A guideline might be weekly visits for the first month, then monthly visits for the next six months, settling to an occasional visit thereafter (the frequency will depend on the degree of need). Pastors cannot do this all themselves, and deacons and elders should be enlisted in this ministry of comfort.

Leadership might also entrust someone to keep a ledger of dates of death and key dates for the mourners such as wedding anniversaries and birthdates of the deceased. Cards, phone calls, flowers, visits, or delivered meals by someone in the church on that date would be a wonderful ministry to these mourners. One particular goal would be to make sure these folks are not alone on the anniversary of the death. Especially during the first year, other impromptu expressions of love and compassion would encourage these brothers and sisters. Keeping their names on prayer lists – again, minimally for the first year – would prompt more intercession for them and keep their loss fresher in the minds of the church.

I believe that we are also a little overprotective of children sometimes when it comes to death. Death comes to everyone, and children will grow to cope with it better if they are not hidden away from it unnecessarily when young. Consider, then, having children come along on visits to those who grieve. Children's classes at the church might make cards or crafts to share with those who mourn. (This may be particularly important if another child is mourning, but children also do very well to learn to care for older adults.)

Given that those who mourn might be tempted to withdraw from social situations and deprive themselves of the burden-bearing benefits of the Christian community, those in the church should consider making special invitation to mourners to come to worship and special events. It may be awkward to walk into a class that is predominantly couples when you are now a widow or widower. Having someone bring you and walk with you through the trip can encourage participation.

The same goes for children who may feel awkward about how they will be treated after a parent or grandparent has died. This may be merited, as children are uninformed about how to deal with friends who are suffering. What a teachable time for them to learn how to empathize with loss and to be a presence of Christ in the lives of their friends. Sunday School and other teachers can capitalize on these opportunities to instruct children about death and grief. Speaking of children, another ministry to mourners is for the church to have someone offer childcare so that grieving parents can have some time together and a brief respite from the responsibilities of parenting.

There are many practical ministries a thoughtful congregation can provide to mourners. Some may need financial assistance, or help moving to a new living situation, or transportation to the grocery store or doctors' appointments. Many widows and widowers need help in repairing things in the home yet may be hesitant to ask for it. An occasional visit by a deacon or handyman from the church may discover ways to help that might go unnoticed otherwise. Similarly, offering an occasional housecleaning, help with meals, or yard work can mean much to those who mourn. Many who grieve need such help and may be overwhelmed by life's demands.

Another service to those who mourn is to offer them a chance to minister to others. Some losses leave the individual with a shattered sense of purpose. For example, if a woman had been caring for a sick husband for several years, she may feel adrift in her life when she no longer is needed for that role. Thoughtful leadership will dispatch someone to discern the gifts of such people and invite them into ministries where their gifts can be used. They may be particularly amenable to helping develop some of the ministries described in this chapter. If nothing else, ask them to pray for the church. I remember a retired missionary in my town that, though aged, would choose an adult theater and sit in her apartment and pray it out of business. When one closed, she would choose another. The theaters never knew what happened! We underestimate the power of prayer, and do well to recruit those who may have more time for prayer. A sense of being needed can be a great encouragement for some who are bereaved.

Maybe the most basic thing to be done is to love the mourners. It is easy to avoid speaking to them at church if we feel awkward about it. Yet, the last thing they need is to feel alienated because of their loss. Step in faith to say 'hello' to mourners in our midst, even if it feels uncomfortable.

Find occasions to invite those who grieve into a conversation about how they are doing. Trite 'How are you doing?' queries are met with the predictable response of 'Fine'. We may then feel pretty smug that we showed our concern and think the person is doing well. Better to find occasion where you have a few minutes and invite more genuine discussion by saying things like, 'I can't imagine what it is like to live without him,' or 'What are some of the hardest times for you?' or 'Can you tell me a specific way I could pray for you?' Hopefully, you get the idea: ask more specific questions and suggest that you assume this is a difficult time.

That can help the person open up to you and afford you more opportunity to minister.

Some churches might even consider having weekly small group meetings for those who have lost loved ones, and there are helpful programs such as Grief Share (www.griefshare.org) available to help structure such an endeavor.

A brief chapter will not allow us to explore all of the ways you can serve those who mourn and in so doing show the 'true religion' that James speaks of. Pray that God will show you and your church other ways to fulfill the ministry to those who mourn, and to avoid superficiality in so doing.

❧ PRAYER ☙

God our Father, thank You for giving us opportunity to
step into others' pain, faintly echoing the way that Jesus
stepped into ours. Grant us grace and power to serve
those around us who mourn.

Witnessing to God's Greatness in the Midst of Death

By this all people will know that you are my disciples,
if you have love for one another.

JOHN 13:35

There are an abundance of theories on why Christians are losing their influence in Western society, and about what we can do to make the church 'relevant' again. For some strange reason, it seems that the theme of many of these is for the church to change to fit the culture. We want music and a worship environment that make people comfortable and for them to leave thinking 'I enjoyed that' rather than 'How great is our God!' Our world is all about our pleasure and happiness, doing what it can to deny any 'unhappy' thoughts. We learned in Part I how this leads to a denial of death and a focus on the present life to the neglect of the life hereafter.

It seems logical to look to Jesus for guidance on how His disciples can catch the world's attention and be 'relevant'. Jesus makes it simple in John 13:35: love one another, and the world will notice. This held true in the early church, as Tertullian is reported to have commented, '"Look," they say, "how they love one another" (for they themselves hate one another); "and how they are ready to die for each other" (for they themselves are readier to kill each other).' In a world of increasing hatred and anger that stems from great self-centeredness, a loving body of Christ will not go unnoticed.

In a way, this entire book can be summarized as thoughts about how we can love God and one another in the midst of the last enemy, death. The denial of death is unmasked, and pleasure is dethroned before an even greater enemy. Christians alone know victory of death, and thus we neither deny nor ignore its pain, yet we also find in it hope that the world cannot know. If we cling to the love of God as we face death, and love one another well in the midst of it, we glorify God in the face of our greatest adversary.

It is not accomplished with platitudes, but with gut-wrenching honesty, lament, burden-bearing, tears, and grief. We need not hide from the pain of death and dying and can face it all the more courageously because of the hope we have in Jesus Christ. Whether we are walking through the valley before a loved one dies, or after, or whether we ourselves are facing our own mortality in the near future, or whether we minister to those we love as they tread these sacred paths, we are controlled by love. We love the one for whom we grieve, and love the ones who grieve for us and with us. But most of all, we love the One who has delivered us from the wages of sin. Death is the entrance into a bliss that we can only taste now.

Shortly after Jesus's comment about how our love will change the world, He gave us a glimpse of what awaits:

> Let not your hearts be troubled. Believe in God; believe also in me. In my Father's house are many rooms. If it were not so, would I have told you that I go to prepare a place for you? And if I go and prepare a place for you, I will come again and will take you to myself, that where I am you may be also. (John 14:1-3)

We may be taken to Jesus soon, or may witness others make that transition before it is our turn. Better yet, we may still be here when He returns for us. However or whenever we get there, our future is living in our Father's house. Because of this astounding hope, we say with confidence,

> O death, where is your victory? O death, where is your sting?
> (1 Cor. 15:55)